The Time is Now

The Time
is Now

Sixty "Time Pieces" for Getting
the Most Out of Every Day

DANIEL S. WOLK

THE OVERLOOK PRESS

WOODSTOCK & NEW YORK

First published in the United States in 1998 by
The Overlook Press, Peter Mayer Publishers, Inc.
Lewis Hollow Road
Woodstock, New York 12498

Library of Congress Cataloging-in-Publications Data

Wolk, Daniel S.
The Time is Now : Sixty "time pieces" for getting the most
out of every day / Daniel Wolk.
p. cm.
1. Conduct of life. 2. Time management. I. Title.
BJ1581.2.W626   1998   97-18330   170'.44—dc 21

BOOK DESIGN AND FORMATTING BY BERNARD SCHLEIFER

Manufactured in the United States of America
ISBN 087951-832-4

First Edition
1 3 5 7 9 8 6 4 2

Acknowledgments

MY APPRECIATION TO

Joel Davis who began the process.

Jane Dystel, my literary agent whose wisdom and faith remain unflagging.

Tracy Carns who edited the broad concept and the individual word.

Margie McCabe who knew the meaning of now and always responded with enthusiasm and expertise.

Sister Mary Campion. Her inspiration transcends her passing.

Friends who responded to my inquiry: "If you only had two years to live, how would you live?"

My wife Marion who has always cared, in times then and now.

La Villette, Chateau Unang, W.F. Albright Institute in Jerusalem—the sites for whatever insights appear in this book.

Contents

Part 3
BE CAREFUL OF THE RUT
YOU CHOOSE
Breaking Old Patterns
89

Part 4
THE ATM AND THE HOURGLASS
Outwitting Time
145

Part 5
LANYARDS
On Weaving Time for Yourself
and for Loved Ones
189

Part 6
YOU ONLY LIVE TWICE
Making the Most of Time
237

Dedication

THIS BOOK IS DEDICATED TO MY FATHER, who, even in his final months, understood the precious gift of life, lived fully in the present and refused to squander any moment of his too brief years.

It was 1956. My father and I sat in the bedroom of our home in Albany, New York, looking out on a mountain ash in the front yard. Birds swooped in and stole the orange berries from the branches of the tree.

"What will you major in?" my father asked.

I was a sophomore in college.

"Literature," I answered. The romantic poets. Byron. Keats. Shelley."

"And after college? What will you do then?"

I looked puzzled.

"Perhaps you wonder why I ask these questions, Daniel, but I wanted you to know, whatever you choose to do in life I will be satisfied—as long as it is right for you."

My father sighed. "I may not be here to see the paths you choose. The reports from Mass. General Hospital were not good. The blood cancer is spreading."

The year was 1956. I was a sophomore in college and my father was dying. He was fifty-eight and dying. The same age as I am now.

Why do I share this story? A story of the death of the one person most important to me for so many years. Why? Because this story is not about death. It is about how my father lived— especially the last year of his life.

Like many of us my father had a dream. He was a rabbi and his dream was to build a sanctuary, a temple designed like a tent in the wilderness. A temple soaring into space; to inspire future generations. For eighty years his congregation, Beth Emeth, had worshipped in downtown Albany, near the state capitol. Now they would erect a new structure on Academy Road.

On a cold October day, my father lifted the first spadeful of dirt at the ceremonial ground breaking; he also carried the weight of the doctor's prognosis. He would die. But this knowledge did not compromise his devotion to ensuring the temple would be built. Day after day he drove to the site, walked barren ground, and watched steel girders slowly rise. As the months passed my father no longer had the strength to wander through the maze of unfinished rooms, but every day a congregant drove him to Academy Road, parked across from the Albany Academy, where I had attended high school, and my father watched the progress. His spirit never waned. With each visit he marked one more accomplishment in the slow emergence of his dream. As the peaked wooden roof inched its way into the heavens my father gave thanks. For what? For his own life. Looking back on that chapter in my family's history I realize my father viewed each steel beam that rose as one more confirmation of his own presence on earth.

When forsythia sent out yellow harbingers of rebirth, of spring, my father lay in bed, planning the dedication ceremony—carefully choosing the words with which he would address the congregation. One week before the event the doctor suggested that my father tape the dedication message. Dad hesitated then said with confidence: "It's not necessary. I will be on that pulpit. I will be there." Finally, he agreed to record his words. They began, "As we consecrate this sanctuary to God. . . ."

The dedication of the Temple was scheduled for May 29th. On the morning of May 29th my father died. Peacefully. And fulfilled.

The Time is Now is not a book about death. Quite the opposite. It is a book about enjoying the wonder of life. My father died at an early age but he never felt he had been deprived or cheated. Even in his final year. Why? Because he viewed life as a constant journey. He treasured the steps leading to the mountain top as much as he might have delighted in reaching the peak. He realized that every moment can be a dream within our grasp.

My father, the product of the immigrant experience, raised in an orphanage, plucked each blossom life offered and realized his dreams over and over. When his time came to leave this earth, and he asked himself, "Where, have I been all my life?" he could answer with a smile, "To many promised lands."

There are those who live to be fifty-eight. Others live to be ninety-five. Some of us die at twenty-five. Not a physical death—a death of the spirit. I would define death as that point in our lives when we no longer savor the wonder of life, no longer experience the promise of a new day, no longer grow. That may occur at any age. *The Time Is Now* urges the reader to look back on the years and to ask: Have I used my time well? Have I, at least once, taken the road less traveled? Have I appreciated each day, found pleasure even in the midst of sadness, observed sunlight filtering through the clouds?

Recently I saw a poster: "This life is a test. It is only a test. If it had been an actual life, you would have received further instructions on where to go and what to do." But this life is not a test. It is all we have. To live richly or to squander.

Where have you been all of your life? Are you satisfied with your answer? Few of us are. But the premise of this book, and each vignette in this book, assumes we can begin today to appreciate our years. Today. Who knows where we might arrive if we set off on the myriad of paths that lie before us; if we open the doors of opportunity calling to us.

> *These woods are lovely, dark and deep,*
> *But I have promises to keep,*
> *And miles to go before I sleep,*
> *And miles to go before I sleep.*

My father lived the last year of his life believing he still had miles to go before he slept. That final sleep. He gained satisfaction with every day that dawned and he knew it is not what you have lost but what you have left that matters. All of us have time left. Could we use that time more productively? Could we gain greater happiness and contentment? Where have I been all my life can lead to the question: "Where do I want to be the rest of my life?"

This book is dedicated to my father, Samuel Wolk, born: 1899–died: 1957, but it is really dedicated to anyone willing to ask: "Where do I want to be in my own life, and with those I love?" Inspired by your own unique answer you can move toward lands filled with promise, personal sanctuaries where your hopes may be realized, where your dreams come to pass.

PART 1

THE CICADA COMPLEX

Begin Your Life Now

The Cicada Complex

When Will You Begin Your Life?

SITTING ON THE DECK of a stately house in suburban New York I heard the whir of wings approaching from a trellis draped with climbing pink roses. It was late at night and only the rising crescendo penetrated the barrier of blackness. We looked at one another and Barry, our host, said: "Cicadas."

"They've been coming every night," Barry explained. "They're all over. Never had them before this summer but whenever we come onto the deck they sense our presence. When I was young, in Israel, I once rode a motor scooter through a plague of locusts—but not in Scarsdale!"

While we spoke the advanced guard swooped in under the beams. Loud chatter announced their flight. Dozens descended, landing on my shoulder, in the sorbet and several, investigating the light, flew too close to the candles, igniting their lacy wings. Aroused by the excitement Barry's black lab, Bingo, placed his paws on the table and snapped at the cicadas. The dish of sorbet slipped onto my lap. Thus ended another intimate dinner party in Scarsdale, New York.

I forgot about the cicadas until, months later, I strolled in the French market at Vaison La Romaine. Positioned between a table of purple garlic and a stand selling linen napkins in the blue and gold colors of Provence, a display featured cicadas mounted behind glass. The tan and brown cicadas were tacked onto a white background and, even mounted, gave off an eerie presence. Who would buy framed cicadas?

I told the owner of the stall of my experience on that evening in the United States. "They flew directly into the flames. I know they're only bugs but still—to snuff out your own life."

The slender man, wearing a suede vest, spread his arms and shrugged. "What do you know about these bugs?" he asked.

"Nothing."

"I will tell you. Cicada live four years underground before they are born. Four years before they rise through layers of dirt. And what happens when they are born? They feed off pine tree sap, breed and die. Three or four months and they die. Rest assured, Monsieur, those cicadas who flew into the flames hardly shortened their lives."

Cynically the Frenchman added, "Not very French, oui? Four years before birth. Three months of life. Where is their savoir faire? Would you wish to imitate the Cicada?"

I answered the question while winding my way through the marketplace. No, I would not wish to imitate the cicada. But I know people who—waiting and waiting for their lives to begin— huddle in dark places, considering what they might be when they spread their wings. Life slips by. Then they emerge. Too late?

Beware of the Cicada Complex. Although Ralph Waldo Emerson never wrote about cicadas he believed, "We are always getting ready to live but we never begin." That might be an accurate description of the Cicada Complex—and of ourselves. For instance, what did you intend to accomplish in the past week? In the past year? Did you? How many of your dreams were attempted? How many times have you said, "In my life I hope to," "I'll do it when the children are older," "Once I establish my professional credentials I'll spend more time with my family." Did you? How would you rank on the scale of the Cicada Complex? A 1? A 5? A 10?

After a discussion of the Cicada Complex a close friend, Beth, wrote

Dear Dan,

I would erase the word "someday" from my vocabulary. Someday I will visit my aunt who lives alone; someday I will finish the family tree and let my children know their origins; someday I will paint the scenes I remember from my childhood on the Maine coast; the mist rising off the ocean near Kennebunk, a heron spreading its giant gray wings over an inland lake. Someday I will tell those closest to me how much I really love them. Someday.

The day I received your letter I found a wonderful quote pinned to the bulletin board at the school where I teach:

God put me on Earth
To accomplish a certain
Number of things.
Right now I am so far behind
I will probably never be allowed to die.

Your letter and those words reminded me of all I have to do; an endless list; but whoever suggested that I will never be allowed to die was wrong. I will be allowed to die. Probably before I am ready. If I intend to make a dent in my list I better start soon. Today. Therefore, I intend to erase the word 'someday' from my vocabulary.

Beth

P.S. I probably won't do this until tomorrow.

"I probably won't do this until tomorrow." Oh, Beth! I know the meaning of those words! For instance, I love the south of France but I don't speak French. When I visit a village market to purchase a sausage for lunch I point, I draw, I sigh, I shake my head, and I end up with a banana instead of a sausage. Imagine a lunch of banana on a baguette! Last year I promised myself I would learn French, but, my "Learn to Speak French" tape remains hidden under our dog Teddy's bag of Milk Bones in the closet. Someday! Someday I will learn French—or at least learn to draw a sausage that doesn't look like a banana! Why can't I put aside one hour a day to learn French? Why don't I make a list of what I want to do and hang the list on the mirror in my bathroom? The list would begin:

"Good morning, Dan. Will you begin French tape number one today? Learn how to turn on the computer? Call for concert tickets?" And at the bottom of the list I would affix the picture of a cicada.

In one of the classics of contemporary literature, *Waiting For Godot*, Vladimir and Estragon wait on a country road for Godot. Who is Godot? God? Time? Whoever, or whatever, Godot offers some form of salvation as evident in this excerpt.

ESTRAGON: Didi.
VLADIMIR: Yes.
ESTRAGON: I can't go on like this.
VLADIMIR: That's what you think.
ESTRAGON: If we parted? That might be better for us.
VLADIMIR: We'll hang ourselves tomorrow. (*Pause*)
Unless Godot comes.
ESTRAGON: And if he comes?
VLADIMIR: We'll be saved.

But Godot doesn't come and the tragicomic pair of Vladimir and Estragon continue to wait by the country road until, in the final lines:

VLADIMIR: Well, shall we go?
ESTRAGON: Yes, let's go.
(*They do not move. Curtain.*)

Waiting. Waiting. Never moving. Waiting to be saved. "They do not move." The curtain is drawn on anyone who does not move. We have one life and only we can decide whether we will spend it laughing or weeping; active participants or spectators. If you save your dreams for someday, your dreams will never be realized. Beware of the Cicada Complex.

Gone Fishin'

Why Are You Waiting to Enter Life?

J OHN LOOKED AT HIS WATCH, shook his head and pulled another beer from the cooler in the bow of the canoe. "Not yet, Dan. Not yet." We were bobbing on the rippling water of the cove near my house at Brant Lake and I tingled with the excitement of catching a monster bass.

Why did I expect success?

Why, when for years I could only catch Charlie the sunfish who hung around my dock and allowed himself to be hooked as a friendly gesture. (House rules insisted I throw Charlie back for my next fishing failure.) I was something of a wimp in the minds of the fish that inhabited Brant Lake. Some fish had even spread the word, "Real fish never bite Dan's hook." Over the years I had become known as a soft touch, supplier of minnows for hungry bass, and a supplier of funds for Ray's bait store. Ray had already sent two sons to college, thanks to my twenty years of buying minnows. Friends scoffed when I went off to "feed the fish."

With John on the scene my fortunes would change. He was a twenty-first century fisherman steeped in devices guaranteed to catch fish. We had loaded his high-tech fish finder into the boat followed by metal line for deep trolling and lures tested at Hubbard Space Center. No, this was not just another fishing day. This was the first day of the rest of my fishing life. Fish beware!

Paddling to the far side of the cove, beyond the beaver dam, I took rod and reel in hand, ready to cast into the lily pads. John rolled up the sleeve of his khaki chamois shirt, looked at his watch and whispered, "Not yet, Dan. Sorry, not yet." Puzzled, I left the minnow dangling by the side of the boat, hoping a passing fish might accidently hook itself, and asked John, "Why? This is a perfect place to fish. Why can't I cast?"

John pointed to his watch, a Casio, encased in thick metal. "This watch," John said, "I bought it last month at the fishing show in Madison Square Garden. It tells the right time to fish."

"Right time?"

"Yep. Certain hours are best for fishing. Depends on the gravitational pull and the latitude. In April 3:00 P.M.'s a perfect time but not now. Not in June. We have to wait."

So we settled back into the canoe, opened a six-pack and waited. Around us fishermen in rowboats and outboards pulled in fish.

"How do you explain his success?" I asked, pointing to a fisherman who had just caught a fine specimen.

"Just a fluke," John replied. But it wasn't a fluke. It was what I estimated as a three-pound bass. Fluke aren't found in Brant Lake. By 5:00 P.M. fish were jumping all over the cove. One especially athletic trout teased me by jumping over the boat.

"Now, John? Now?" I asked as the sun began to set. Salivating I stroked my fishing rod. John looked at his watch and then shook his head. "Wait. Wait, oh ye of little faith." Not only was he stealing my pleasure, John was also stealing my lines.

Finally, John looked at his Casio and with solemnity befitting a state occasion announced. "It is 7:30. The time has come. Cast, Dan, cast."

"7:30!" I yelled. "I promised Marion we would be back by 7:30. We have an 8:00 dinner reservation at Friends Lake Inn. Paddle, John, paddle. We're heading home! Maybe we'll fish tomorrow." But "tomorrow" blew up into a furious storm and we were reduced to remaining in the cabin and playing "Go Fish" with the children. Late in the day John packed his fish finder, rods, and lures and went home.

After that abortive attempt at fishing by the watch I lost track of John until one day I met him on the train to White Plains. "How's fishing by the Casio?" I called. John laughed. "Last summer the battery ran down. Haven't replaced it. Now I fish at any hour. You should see the large mouth I caught in Kensico Reservation—worth stuffing and hanging on the wall."

He added. "If you know anyone who wants a Casio fishing watch, have them call me."

I left the train station realizing I had been hooked on John's theory that there is a correct time to fish. Even he had admitted his error. If you wait until 7:30 it may be too late. Cast! Enter the waters of Brant Lake! Enter the waters of life! Otherwise you will never catch what's out there.

The best time to cast? The best time to live? Now!

And that's for reel!

Unless we cast, not only into the waters of a northern lake but into life, we will never catch our desires, fulfill our lives. John had put me on hold but no one puts time on hold. In the first century a disciple living in Jerusalem asked his teacher, Hillel: "What is the right time to act? Should I wait?"

In return Hillel asked, "If not now, when?"

An updated translation of, "If not now, when?" is the ad for Nike sneakers, "Just Do It." Cast. Live. There is never a perfect moment to enter the flowing waters of life. And, in the pastoral mood of this piece: "He who wants milk should not sit on a stool in the middle of the pasture expecting the cows to back up to him."

This spring I entertained house guests, a pair of barnswallows who chose my garage for a six-week rendezvous with parenting. They constructed a mud and spittle nest in a beam over my white Toyota (which quickly became off-white). Soon babies chirped and the proud parents of quads scavenged back and forth bringing baby food. Worms and insects.

The day the barnswallows embarked into the real world mom, dad, and the kids swung on a wire strung across the garage (a warm-up exercise), then flew to their future, but one baby remained behind, huddled in the nest. The mother bird flew in and out, chirping in a language I could not understand but the meaning was obvious: "Come on, fly. You can't stay in that nest forever." (Which was true since we already had a hose ready to clean out their home.") "Fly! It's time to go! Fly!" Finally, the baby flew.

The nest has disappeared but the mother's wise counsel lingers on "Fly! It's time to go. Get on with life!"

Often fear holds us back. What will we find when we venture out? No one can answer that question, but usually we flourish once we step into the world.

> *"Come to the edge," he said.*
> *They said: "We are afraid."*
> *"Come to the edge," he said.*
> *They came.*
> *He pushed them,*
> *And they flew.*
>   (GUILLAUME APOLLINAIRE)

If no one pushes us, we need to push ourselves.

When I was a sophomore in college, Robert Frost addressed the student body. His words floated over rows of pews in the old stone chapel.

> *These woods are lovely, dark, and deep,*
> *but I have promises to keep,*
> *and miles to go before I sleep,*
> *and miles to go before I sleep.*

He paused and a voice asked, "Mr. Frost, what do you mean by that verse?" A slight smile crept over the poet's weathered face. "Someday you will understand." The years have passed and now I understand. We have promises to keep. Promises to ourselves to savor the precious gift of life. Promises to fulfill before the sleep of a single night or the sleep of eternity. Unless we enter the woods, the meadow, and the valleys those promises will never be realized.

Fulfill the promise of your life. Cast. Now.

Heron Watching

Time Cannot Be Captured

"Have Nikon will travel!"

Janet never went anywhere without a camera, but on this biting October morning all she had on her shoulder was a yellow down parka. The smell of wet pine needles and the smoke from cedar logs smoldering in the stone fireplace drifted over the dock where we stood, watching the mist gently rise.

Suddenly, from the cove where otters live, a giant grey heron soared over the rocky point and landed on the bow of a canoe twenty feet away. The heron tucked in its wings and scanned the lake. Although I often saw the heron, wings spread majestically, fly over the camps at the far end of the lake, the bird seldom visited our home. Softly I said to Janet, "Look, look at the beauty of that heron." But Janet had disappeared, racing up the path to the house.

For several minutes the heron, net crooked, stared at the water until, frightened by the sound of a branch falling into the lake, the bird spread its wings and soared toward a sky dotted with gray storm clouds. Soon the bird had vanished over lily pads where red and yellow leaves reflected in the glassy water. The moment the bird disappeared Janet reappeared, her presence announced by the creaking planks of the dock. This time her camera bag hung loosely on one arm.

"The heron," she stammered, "where's the heron?"

"Gone," I replied. "Somewhere in the lily pads. Wasn't it beautiful?"

Janet stared in the direction of the lily pads but all she saw was a lone fisherman.

Sadly Janet rested the camera on the dock. "Dan, whenever I'm prepared, camera in hand, the scene never materializes. The night of an eclipse it rains. On a photographic safari in East Africa I picked the one week the lions were on vacation. When you said, 'Janet, we might see a beautiful gray heron that occasionally soars over this end of the lake' I thought of bringing my camera but then I thought, 'Not a chance,' and left the camera in the house. The moment the heron circled I ran into the house. Never saw the heron. Missed the action."

I smiled. "Janet, why did you have to photograph the heron? Why couldn't you just stand here? Watch the beauty? Even for a moment?"

Janet sighed. "I'm not sure, Dan. I guess I wanted to capture that moment forever. On film. I don't know. But why couldn't the heron wait?"

Because, Janet, I thought, that's the way herons are. Not very considerate birds. But I knew that wasn't the reason the heron did not wait. We cannot capture a bird in flight and I felt sorry for Janet. Not because she missed the heron. The Adirondacks are filled with glorious pictures. I felt sorry for Janet because she had attempted to stop time instead of acknowledging that, like a bird in flight, life is in constant flux; to be enjoyed as it passes, not to be immortalized.

The philosopher Santyana wrote, "To be interested in the changing seasons is a happier state of mind than to be hopelessly in love with spring."

If only we could stop time. We cannot. And, when we try, life passes us by. We miss the awakening of spring, the warmth of summer, the autumn hues, a landscape painted white with snow. Youth. Middle age. The rich harvest of the years. The wise heron enjoys my dock in summer before migrating south when the chill winds descend from Canada. Life is a migration from moment to moment.

In his autobiography *Report To Greco*, Nikos Kazantzakis describes his search for meaning, a quest that takes him from a monastery at the foot of Mt. Sinai to a Buddhist temple in Japan. In his latter years he returns to his native Greece and meets with Zorba, a peasant who mocks Kazantzakis' search for ultimate answers. For Zorba life unfolds in dancing on a beach and he invites Kazantzakis to join him. Kazantzakis accepts.

> *Come on Zorba, teach me to dance. Zorba leaped to his feet, his face sparkling. 'To dance, Boss? To dance? Fine! Come on!'*
> *Off we go then, Zorba! My life is changed!*

Zorba understood the dance of life; the need to rejoice in the moment. To lift our feet on the sands of time and enjoy what is close at hand.

Time moves too swiftly to delay. If you ever question this truth visit New York City. The Tourneau Building on the corner of 34th and Seventh Avenue to be exact. A digital clock spans the face of this building. White numbers race across a black backdrop before tumbling off the screen and vanishing in the air. 4:47:36:9. Four o'clock, forty-seven minutes, thirty-six seconds and nine tenths of a second. Blink in the bright sunlight and when you look again the clock records 4:47:38:11. What is the purpose of a clock recording tenths of seconds? Perhaps to awaken passersby to the swift movement of time.

Time cannot be stopped. Flow. Flow with time. Do you want to miss the heron?

Turn the Handle

Open Doors of Opportunity

S IX MONTHS BEFORE I LEFT for France the owner of La Villette sent me the keys to the house. "The front door has two locks; use this key for the upper lock, this one for the lower. The other keys will be in the kitchen hanging above the stove."

I arrived at the eighteenth century villa in the season when cherries were still golden and poppies peeked out from the stone dry walls. In the distance the abandoned castle of Montbrun Les Bain ruled the countryside, its ruins caressed by the evening sun. The double wooden door of La Villette swung open stiffly. I entered a room with low slung beams and windows overlooking the valley. The old shutters swung in the mistral and I pictured the original tenants, a young farming family indentured to Lord Montbrun, seeking refuge from the strong winds.

In the 1990s La Villette was rented to visitors seeking an unspoiled vacation in rustic Provence. Those wishing to spend two weeks among fields of lavender could stay in a house where the American owners had assured every comfort, including explicit directions.

"Quilts are in the master bedroom across from the dovecote."

One wall of the gabled master bedroom was lined with hundreds of niches where doves had nested. I hoped the homing pigeons had relinquished rights to their ancestral home.

Instructions continued: How to contact M. Isnard, the electrician, M. Arnoux, the plumber, and the laundress A. Quinlen, whose colloquial French increased in speed once she learned we did not understand a word. There were times when plumber, electrician, and cleaning lady descended on the cottage at the same time. I feared one day I would turn on the upstairs faucet and the lights would go off in the living room.

Slipping away from the pages of instructions I escaped into the kitchen to search for the keys to my temporary kingdom. There they were! Dangling above shelves filled with olive oil, purple garlic, and wine. Some of the keys were shiny and silver, others encrusted with layers of rust; the type of key normally found in a village flea market. Marion left for a walk into town on trails flanked by purple iris while I inspected storage closets, fuse boxes, and doors opening into cavernous stone areas off the lower level. Vanishing into dark, musty places I explored piles of firewood, an ox yoke, a sleigh, and ancient cherry pickers. Some doors, warped over time, presented a challenge but by late afternoon I had conquered La Villette.

With one exception. The door of an old stone barn across a narrow grass courtyard refused to yield its secret. Several keys fit but none of them would turn the latch. A distant cuckoo mocked my efforts. In the days that followed I often attempted to open the door, sometimes sneaking up unannounced. The lock refused to budge.

Our vacation over, Marion and I prepared to leave La Villette. On that last bittersweet morning, Christine, a charming friend of La Villette's owners, arrived to cut the lawn. "I came from Avignon," she explained in a melodic French, then, realizing we were not "so very French" she spoke in English. "You enjoyed your stay at La Villette? No?" We described our love of the delightful chateau, returned to our packing, and listened to the sound of the lawnmower in the background.

Before we left I indulged in a farewell tour of the property. The cherries had turned red, ready for harvesting, and green figs hung from the trees on the north side of the house. Passing the barn I stopped short—the door, that elusive door, was open and merrily swinging on its hinges. "Hey!" I yelled. Christine, assuming I was in pain rushed over. "Monsieur?"

"The door is open," I gasped.

"Certainly. That is where I keep the lawnmower."

"Then you have the only key that works?"

"Key?" Christine replied.

"Yes," I exclaimed. "For two weeks I tried to open that door. None of my keys worked."

Christine looked puzzled. "That door does not have a key. Just lift the metal wire. Like this." In a matter of seconds she had opened and closed the door several times. Then, seeing the keys swinging from my belt, she laughed, "Not every room at La Villette needs a key. This door was never locked."

Eagerly I approached the one unexplored section of La Villette. My eyes acclimated to the darkness of a small room with a blackened hearth stretching across the back walls. Beams criss-crossed the ceiling at different levels.

"Christine, what was this room?"

"Centuries ago, when La Villette was only a farm, this was the bakery. On the lower beams the farmer stored long wooden spoons. He used the spoons to place dough on the hearth and to turn the loaves."

For Christine the barn room stored her tractor, lawnmower, and well aged wine vats but my imagination drifted back to a hardened Provencal farmer bundling up on chilly mornings and gathering wood from dead grapevines or oak branches to stoke his fire. I could smell the warm bread filling the early morning air.

Bidding the hearth farewell I left La Villette, but not before evaluating the morning's events. What if I had never discovered the hearth? As I watched the road sign "Montbrun Les Bains" grow faint I felt the pleasure of uncovering a two hundred-year-old secret. The warmth of the past, the fragrance of bread baking was La Villette's parting gift to enrich my senses wherever I traveled.

Once more I heard Christine's words: "Not every room at La

Villette needs a key—not *every* room." How many other doors have I passed, convinced I could not enter? How many roads not taken, opportunities neglected, paths unexplored?

Ever since La Villette, when I pass a closed door, I hear Christine's laughing voice from a freshly mowed field in the south of France. "Monsieur, not every room at La Villette needs a key. This door was never locked." Never locked. Never locked. Never locked.

Franz Kafka tells of a man who spent his life sitting by the gate of a castle, waiting for the gate to open. In his final days he hobbles up to the gatekeeper. "When is this gate open?" The keeper of the gate responds: "Open? My good man, this gate is always open—to those who approach. Tell me friend, why did you sit by the roadside all these years instead of entering?"

La Villette and Kafka urge me to take advantage of opportunities. Life is a tabula rasa, an unpainted landscape awaiting our imprint. Life is *Moby Dick*'s white whale seeking our interpretation. The years that stretch before us overflow with possibilities, but only if we take advantage of those possibilities. Have you watched children playing in a fresh snowfall? Sometimes they lie down in the snow and stretch out their arms. When they stand up the impression of an angel graces the snow. At any age we might benefit by leaving our own imprints on a new snowfall; a warmup for the marks we could place on our lives.

Several years ago I sat in a plane on a distant runway at Westchester Airport. We had taxied out but a heavy fog prohibited us from taking off. After breakfast, peanut snacks and three Coca-Colas, I looked at my watch. 10:00 A.M. Zero visibility. Why didn't we return to the terminal? Suddenly the pilot's triumphant voice announced: "Fasten seat belts," and we were aloft. With pride the pilot continued. "We apologize for the delay. We are now on our way to Chicago." Then, unable to resist, he added, "Incidentally, the fog has descended again. Those planes that returned to the terminal have canceled their flights. We caught the brief break in the clouds. Thank you for flying United!" Those words were not an advertisement for United Airlines. They were the inspiration to be ready when a door opens. Who knows the duration of the opportunity?

Why are we hesitant to venture out? Because most of us prefer the safety of the known over the unfamiliar. André Gide said: "One doesn't discover new lands without consenting to lose sight of the shore for a very long time." Ships may be safe in a harbor but ships were intended to leave their ports. What would happen if a ship never cut loose from its mooring? People also need to cut loose. Robert Kennedy believed: "Only those who dare to fail greatly can ever achieve greatly."

Ask yourself, "If I could not fail what would I do? What door handles would I turn? And if I fail what have I really lost?" What opportunities have you passed by in recent days? What opportunities have passed you by? Can you reduce the number in the six months that lie ahead?

If we try and do not succeed time will assuage our regrets. Time will not assuage regrets for doors we did not open, doors calling to us.

Open doors. You own the key.

Everything's Coming up Cherries

Harvest Opportunity

A BRIEF HISTORICAL NOTE. January 13, 1938 I was born in General Hospital, Wilkes-Barre, Pennsylvania to a family of cherry lovers. Since a love of cherries is a proven genetic trait, I am the newest generation to imbibe cherries.

At one time a genealogist attempted to discover the origins of the family predilection for cherries. Did it come from my mother's Litvak side of the family? My father's origin in Galicia? So far we have not unearthed the roots of this pithy mystery. But this much is known: When cherry season dawned my mother, Mary C. Wolk, could be found bustling down market aisles searching for cherries. Not an easy task in Albany, New York. Oh, yes, cherries flooded the market—but *good* cherries? A scarce commodity. Some bore scars from rough treatment in packing; others inherited little creatures wiggling in and out; some were too ripe, others not ripe enough.

Why do I share this background? Because I trust a personal insight into my family will explain the ecstasy I experienced, when, in the south of France, I sojourned in a cherry orchard. I sat on the patio of an ancient chateau and looked out on rows of cherry trees painted deep red by nature and without blemish. However, the proprietors of the chateau did not care about cherries; their interest lay in grapes. Vineyards stretched from the stone statues in the courtyard to the distant dry riverbed that wound through the gorge and on to the medieval village of Venasque.

One day, I asked my host, Marie-Helene: "Who will pick the cherries?"

"No one," she answered.

'What will happen?"

Marie-Helene shrugged. "Nothing. The birds will eat some. Others will dry up. The trees in the orchard near the gate are already shriveled."

This was more than I could bear. Stretching in front of me were sufficient cherries to feed Albany, Wilkes-Barre, and possibly the whole of Galicia and Lithuania. Going to waste! Mornings I wandered from tree to tree, clinically depressed. Even the cheerful notes of the cuckoo bird singing in the distance failed to lift my spirits. One morning I took control of my life and, with confident step, headed off for the cherry orchard accompanied by Tara, a German shepherd, who also loved cherries with a passion that convinced me Tara, in a previous incarnation, came from Galicia, not Germany. I gorged myself on cherries, disdaining the delicate French food at the chateau. Filled with missionary zeal I brought back baskets heaped with cherries. Standing on an empty wooden carton I cried out to guests peacefully sipping coffee: "Forsake your plans to travel to Paris, the Riviera, Barcelona. Come with me to the cherry orchard and be saved!" I outlined an intricate proposal to harvest cherries, preserve cherries, make jam, bake tarts and export them worldwide. No one bit into my "Save The Cherry, Save Yourself" campaign. Marie-Helene politely pulled me to one side and asked me to stop preaching in public. "We do have a ninth century chapel on the property—If you wish to use the pulpit!" Channeling my energy I opened a cherry stand on Route D4 in front of the chateau, selling cherryade for one franc. Unfortunately every farm in the neighborhood grew cherries and passersby smiled politely before hurrying on.

After returning from France, I finally grasped the meaning of the cherry odyssey while shopping in the fruit department of the A & P. There are periods when life hangs barren. Few pickings.

There are also seasons when promise dangles before us, the fruit of life waiting harvest. At such times why stand back and permit opportunities to wither? Why?

This is the question asked by a lover of cherries who traces his origins from the branches of a cherry tree in France to vanished roots in Lithuania and Galicia.

Statistics affirm that most of us only use ten percent of our potential. What percentage of the opportunities that stretch out before us do we experience? Probably less than ten percent. If there are many doors opening on our lives, a corollary asserts that few of us enter these doors. We pass them by. For instance, over many years I went on bicycle trips pedaling furiously (and futilely) on a three-speed Schwinn. Technology remains anathema to me and I resisted the pressure to buy a more sophisticated bike. Voila! I finally purchased a spiffy orange 21-speed mountain bike but, with regret, I admit that I still only use three speeds. Am I unique? Few of us use all the gears we have. They wither on the tree of life.

At a photography seminar I listened to an introduction of the adventure photographer Nevada Weir. A paraphrase: "Not too long ago Nevada received a letter from a man who had joined her on one of her trips. When he returned home he resumed his routine, uninteresting pattern. Now he looks back on that one trip he took with Nevada. The sights he saw. The photographs he took. The people he met. The cultures he explored—and he regrets the many roads he never took." The moderator paused. "I now take pleasure in introducing Nevada Weir who will never have to say 'There was a road not taken.' She has harvested the fullness of her years."

We do not have to embark on adventure travel to distant lands for life to be a constant adventure. Near the scene of my cherry picking escapades a highway rotary branches off in four directions. Venasque, Carpentras, Pernes and Malemort. To return home I take the Malemort exit but this summer, as an experiment, I turned off onto every exit. To see where the roads would lead. On the road to Pernes I watched the harvesting of yellow plums.

On the road to Carpentras a field of sunflowers turned to watch me pass. On the hill leading to Venasque I visited a medieval castle. Most of us do not have the time to purposely investigate every road but when possible I love to travel on the road not taken. Instead of driving 70 MPH on I95, follow US1 or shore roads. There is always a different way to travel through your life. The rungs of a ladder were never meant to rest upon. Instead they should challenge you to rise higher.

The Talmud, a compendium of Jewish law and ethics, cautions, "On Judgement Day a person will be called into account for every permissible thing he might have enjoyed but did not." Today is judgment day. You are the judge.

Building a Mountain Out of an Ash

Plan for Tomorrow

W HEN DID I FIRST NOTICE THE MOUNTAIN ASH, lip-shaped green leaves, orange berries holding sway over our front yard in Albany, New York? When? I suppose the day I received my driver's license and backed into the tree, leaving a dent in the fender of my parent's new Plymouth. In an act of penitence I vowed, when I owned my own house, to plant a mountain ash, a reminder to navigate life carefully.

Many years later, at age thirty-six, I toured nurseries in Westchester County. "A mountain ash?" the nursery man asked. "They're not popular any more, like cocker spaniels." I missed the point. "Why not buy a Japanese maple or an ornamental cherry tree?" he suggested.

Then, on a back road in horse country, I found a small nursery advertising "Mountain Ash. 3 feet tall." Remembering the twenty-foot-high specimen on South Main Avenue, I asked the salesman, "How long before the mountain ash will reach twenty feet?" He laughed. "Fellow, you'll be an old man before that tree grows to twenty feet. Probably won't even have berries for five or six years. Buy one of those forsythia bushes. They grow like weeds."

I asked my neighbor, an old Yankee who spent summers growing tomatoes and shooting woodchucks, "Burt, how long do you think it would take for a three-foot mountain ash to reach a

respectable height?" Burt was more discouraging than the nurs-
eryman "Forever, Dan. Trees grow slowly. See that row of peach
trees? I planted them five years ago. This is the first year they bore
fruit. And those grapes growing over the deck? I planted them
seven years ago." I stared at the vines. Only a few clusters of
grapes were visible.

"You'll be an old man," Burt repeated, "Probably seven years
before you have a good sized mountain ash."

Seven years! I was already thirty-six. I couldn't wait.

Twenty years have passed. If I had planted a three foot mountain ash twenty years ago my yard would be shaded by broad
limbs. Why didn't I plant for the future? Seven years may seem
like forever but tomorrow is almost now. Sow trees, thoughts,
love—today. Let them grow.

Let's see. I'm fifty-eight. If I plant a mountain ash this
spring. . . .

Time slips by. The future quickly becomes the present and we
wonder, "What have I done to prepare for this moment?"
Tomorrow is almost here.

A young cousin, Matthew, educated me concerning a child's
view of time. He related a trip he had taken with his family including explicit details of how many times he was carsick on the drive
between San Francisco and Los Angeles.

"What else do you remember about the trip, Matthew?"

"Nothing."

"Nothing?"

"Nothing. It was last year. I was only three."

For a four-year-old child, one year is a long time ago. But for
most of us one year is not far away—or five years or twenty-five
years.

If we successfully anticipate the future, we plan for that
future today, but often tomorrow looms far away and we become
easily discouraged. To counter this tendency I recommend the
Jogger's Journey Through Life, a regimen initiated fifteen years
ago when I began jogging and became a huffing, puffing creature

inhaling exhaust fumes and nursing bad knees ostensibly to improve my health. My neighbor jogged six miles daily but I began with a more modest goal, a half mile. On my maiden run I threw in the jogging shorts after three telephone poles. Determined to succeed, I set myself a challenge. Five telephone poles on day two. One hundred after the second week. Now I jog 1,375 telephone poles, which improves my agility and fine-tunes my ability to speed count!

You don't have to be a jogger to subscribe to the Jogger's Journey Through Life. Simply work toward goals in small increments. If you want to paint don't apply for a commission to redo the Sistine Chapel. Start with a small canvas. Plant paper-white bulbs that emerge overnight instead of a mountain ash. Why deny yourself immediate satisfaction? Think small! To remind myself of the potential in small steps I keep an acorn on my study desk. Someday, if I plant that acorn, a majestic oak will shade the lawn. What incredible potential in a little acorn! If the oak resides in the acorn, if a bird sleeps in an egg, what promise lies latent within each moment.

The poet William Blake suggested that we can see the world in a grain of sand. Possibly not an entire world but we can certainly learn from a grain of sand. Walk on a beach, look carefully at a sand dune. What is that dune? Millions of grains of sand stacked one upon the other, ineffectual by themselves but when gathered together a force able to restrain mighty waves. Life consists of minutes stacked one upon the other. If they slip away untended the future will be here with little to show for the passage of time. Build on those minutes now; fashioned with care they will result in goals that can bring satisfaction.

The way to prepare for tomorrow is to use this day correctly.

Watchless in the Sinai

Live Life Instead of Monitoring Life

THOSE WHO SAY THERE ARE MYSTERIES to be discovered in the desert are correct. In the barrenness of the Sinai I finally learned why my watchband always breaks on vacation. But that was well into the trip to the oasis of Ayn Umm Ahmad with Clinton B., an expert on bedouin affairs. When we departed from our camp on the Red Sea the watch was still attached to my wrist.

I climbed into the red jeep whose odometer had stopped at 180,000 miles and took my place beside the bedouin driver. He wore a black and white kefiyah and a red T-shirt with the logo, "Dive Sinai." I glanced at my watch and asked Clinton, "How long before we arrive at Ayn Umm Ahmad?" He laughed. "Who knows? This is the desert. Put away your watch." The time was 10:30 A.M.

At 11:15 A.M. I understood what he meant. The jeep over-heated. For the first time. While I was sitting under a piercing sun waiting for the motor to cool a bedouin woman joined me, crossed her legs and puffed on a cigarette hidden behind a black veil. The driver poured murky water rippling with a swarm of creatures from a jerrycan into the radiator. This was also our drinking water. I patted my bottle of water purification tablets. The time was 12:00 noon. Clinton told me to put away my watch.

The jeep jerked ahead, through sand ruts and over red rocks. We punctured a tire. The time was 1:45 P.M. Clinton told me to put away my watch. At 3:30 we straggled into the oasis where Anez Abu Salam, a bedouin poet, lived. Clinton presented the sheik with new sandals from the Jerusalem market. Anez dropped his old scuffed sandals on the edge of a dune, to be buried by time and I slipped my name and phone number into one of the sandal's leather thongs. In 5,000 C.E., when a descendant of Indiana Jones excavates, he will uncover leather straps bearing strange hiero-glyphics, 9 1/2, 10, 10 1/2, and my name. Entombed for posterity. The time was 4:45 P.M. Clinton told me to put away my watch.

At 4:47 my watch band broke and the watch fell into a bowl of pita bread dough. I was not surprised. My watch bands always break on vacation. The last occasion was climbing the Himalayas, the time before in the carpet market of Kabul, Afghanistan, and once my watch fell under the wheel of a London taxi. Timex's Law: When I travel my watch band breaks. The time was?

Clinton urged. "Now, put your watch away." I stuffed it into my backpack. "Look," he pointed to a young girl leading a flock of sheep, silhouetted against a purple mountainside on the far side of the wadi. "Learn from her," he said. "Each morning that child of twelve, maybe thirteen, is swallowed by the wilderness. Alone on a landscape that has remained unchanged from the time of Moses. Does she live by a watch? Or by the rhythm of the ages?"

At night the Milky Way, Pleiades and Orion found their eter-nal place in the heavens. Listening to the steady drone of bedouin voices around the campfire, "Aie Wa, Aie Wa," "Yes, Yes" I drifted off to sleep. Released from time.

On the return trip to Jerusalem, leaning against a stack of watermelon, I watched a camel loping alongside the jeep and this time, when smoke poured from the engine, I sat calmly. Legs crossed. Like a bedouin. As we turned onto the road out of the wilderness of Sinai, Clinton prodded me. "How is life without a watch? Did you exist?"

I existed. Twenty-four hours without saying, "I'm too late," "I'm running out of time," "When will we arrive?" For a brief peri-od I had lived life instead of monitoring life. What a sense of exhilarating freedom!

A confession: Shortly after leaving the Sinai I purchased a brown leather watch band guaranteed to last forever. You see, some of us never learn. Even with time!

In the 1990s we are governed by time; perhaps we are victims of time. This is evidenced in the watches we wear, the filofaxes we carry, the computerized memory banks in our suit pockets, the memos on Post-Its. We are the programmed generation. Even my dog Teddy can not escape dragging along a heavy schedule at the end of her leash; hair grooming at Wags and Whiskers on Tuesday, heartworm pill on Wednesday, a long walk on Thursday. We are either too late, or too early (seldom), scurrying along the streets of New York, zigzagging in and out of the streets of suburbia. Going. Coming.

In the nineteenth century James Truslow Adams commented, "Perhaps it would be a good idea, fantastic as it sounds, to muffle every telephone and halt all activity for an hour some day to give people a chance to ponder for a few moments on what it is all about, why they are living and what they really want." But could we exist without the pressures of time? From Moses to Thomas Merton people retreated to the desert to commune with themselves. Unhindered by time. Watchless in the Sinai. But this phenomena can cause anxiety.

When I was a rabbinical student we were granted the option of conducting a creative service. One of my classmates experimented with a modified Quaker service. His philosophy was to help us forget worldly concerns. Sit in solitude and silence. After three or four minutes the congregation shifted uneasily. After five minutes we quietly disappeared. Program me! I thought. Tell me what to say, what page to read, when to rise and when to sit.

Time controls our lives. For instance, we pick up one child at 2:30, the other at 4:00; we watch the 6 o'clock news (if we caught the 5:03 from Grand Central); and so on, and so on. Even when we relax and take a country walk, we review our business deal from the day before and mentally prepare for Monday morning. Once clocks did not exist. How did a knight in armor, living in the fifteenth century, ever make the 3:13 from London to King Arthur's Court to rescue a damsel in distress and bring her back to the castle on the 5:30 Lancelot Express?

Occasionally we need the opportunity to drift like a leaf blowing in the wind. Otherwise we can not fully participate in the richness of life. Narrowly circumscribed by where we have to be and when we have to be there, we are not responsive to the unexpected, to the flow of the moment.

Therefore, I have made a personal vow. When my watch runs down I will refuse to replace the battery. For two days I will go watchless. What can happen? I'll miss the 11:10 from Rye to New York? No problem. I'll take the 11:40. I'll be late to officiate at a wedding? Being late for a wedding will probably not enhance my reputation but, since love is eternal, the actual fallout should not be grave! Unfortunately this experiment with time will not occur for more than a year. A decal on the back of my Swiss Army watch announces: "Change battery January, 1999."

A more modest proposal. Try leaving your watch at home for one day. If timid about being timeless choose a vacation day. You will be free to concentrate on the moment, appreciate where you are now. Colors, words, emotions will be sharper and more immediate.

A postscript to this modest proposal. On the day you choose to go watchless leave your cellular phone at home. Otherwise a well meaning friend may call to share the time of day.

Let Go of the Ring

On Moving Beyond the Past

I WAS 18 WHEN MY FATHER DIED. On a spring day when roses opened his eyes closed. What do I remember of his life? That throughout the far too brief years we were together he wore a gold ring and matching gold cufflinks. His initials "S.W.", Samuel Wolk, were engraved on the gold surface of the ring and on both cufflinks. After his death I inherited the ring and, as I slipped the ring on my finger, I felt my father's presence. He was there. With me.

Several weeks after the funeral I went swimming in a little pond near Albany. As I sat next to the pond the ring fell off in the grass at my feet but I could not find the ring. Each day a friend and I returned to the side of the pond—searching. I refused to let go of that connection with my father. After days of searching my friend gently counseled, "Dan, stop looking. The ring is gone. It is gone."

Time passed and one day my mother came into my room. "Daniel," she said, "You will not bring back what you have lost. But here. . . ." and she handed me a navy blue jewelry box. Inside was a ring with those precious initials "S.W." Not the original ring. No, that was lost. Forever. But my mother had taken one of the matching cufflinks, also inscribed "S.W.", and mounted the cufflink on my grandfather's gold band.

At that moment I understood a reality of moving beyond

death. Those we love die; dreams evaporate in the light of reality; hopes drift away. Longing for what is gone is a striving after the wind, a journey into emptiness. A day dawns when we must let go.

However, we need not completely relinquish what has gone before. We can build upon the past, a cufflink on a grandfather's gold band. I still wear the ring shaped from my father's cufflinks. The initials "S.W.", barely visible, have worn smooth with time but I have built on this foundation. There are moments when I excavate fragments of my father's presence from the treasure house of memory but I know I will never bring him back.

It is common to live in the past. This tendency traces back to biblical times and a woman named Mrs. Lot. (The Bible refers to her as Lot's wife but in our gender sensitive world I prefer "Mrs. Lot.") The Lots lived in the corrupt city of Sodom, home of, among other vices, sodomy. God decided to destroy Sodom but granted dispensation to Lot and his family. "Lot, you, your wife, your children (the whole *lot* of you) may leave town." God continued: "There is one qualifier. When you leave do not look back." Everyone obeyed except Mrs. Lot. Sodom represented her past. How could she leave? Distraught, she stood on a knoll and cast one last look at her beloved home.

The rest is history. Mrs. Lot turned into a pillar of salt, to be seen on all guided tours of the Dead Sea. What really happened to Mrs. Lot. A miracle? A volcanic eruption that covered her with lava? I prefer a symbolic interpretation. Those who are rooted to the past are immobile as pillars of salt.

Do you suffer from the Mrs. Lot syndrome? Do you always look back and glorify the good old times? Do you tell the same stories over and over while your spouse smiles patiently? Do you remember your college years as "the best years of my life," instead of saying, "These are the best years of my life, the years I am living now." Does the past seem to be a romantic refuge from the present? If you have answered "yes" to the above questions you suffer from the Mrs. Lot syndrome. Curable if caught in time.

Recently, I saw a package of cocktail napkins with the

inscription, "How Can I Be Nostalgic When I Can't Remember Anything?" But we do remember and often we dwell in that memory. We continue to search for the lost ring instead of taking what went before and building upon this base. David Ben Gurion suggested a proper balance between past and present when he said, "The past lives in us, not we in the past."

Once, a reader of the esteemed British magazine *Punch* addressed the editor. "Sir, your magazine is not what it once was."

The editor replied, "And it never was"

On a visit to the Dordogne region of southern France I visited a little village which seemed, at first glance, to be like any small town in the south of France; the ubiquitous patisserie with women in shawls and men in berets scurrying in and out, purchasing a baguette or croissant; the alimentarie with everything from ribbons to sausage. On the main square women kneaded their laundry in the village fountain and shared gossip. Two old-timers played boulé, rolling the metal balls against a stone wall where red poppies pushed their way out of cracks.

The scene might have been found in hundreds of villages. With one exception. Off a back alley, hidden behind a field of sunflowers, an artist worked in his studio. Occasionally a visitor peered beyond the red shutters into the window. In one corner a man sat at a table cluttered with parts from timepieces: the hour hand of a pocket watch, the casing of a grandfather clock, a brass pendulum. On the floor pieces of wood, sea shells, metal rims, a bicycle tire casually surrounded the table legs. Each piece served a purpose for this artist who was, a sculptor of time. A sign announced: "Time: Before you are born it is waiting for you. When you are born it is your birthright. When you die it abandons you like the ivy which dies where it is cut." Beneath the sign, on dusty shelves, the sculptor had assembled collages made out of watches, clocks, and the odds and ends he collected. Each piece made a statement on time. I concentrated on a clock constructed out of a conch shell and a weathered chunk of drift wood. The wood represented a launching pad for the shell carved in the shape of a space ship. Instead of hands moving forward, the hands of this clock moved backward. 4:00 P.M., 3:00 P.M., 2:00 P.M. At the base of the clock the sculptor had written

> *A tribute to Einstein's theory of relativity.*
> *As a matter of convention, when the hands of a clock turn to the right, you are getting older. If you look at the model before you, you will note that the hands turn in the opposite direction, so that as you watch you are getting younger.*

What would happen if I could turn the hands of time back? I could jog without muscles stiffening. How else would I, could I, change my life? But why speculate? I cannot go backwards. A sculptor of clocks can create hands to move in reverse; the creator of time did not offer this option. Take your past, treasure your past but recognize that at one time the past was the present. To instill meaning in this past implies appreciating today.

The cycle of life goes on. You will never find the ring from years gone by.

PART 2

EVEN A WATCH THAT DOESN'T WORK . . .

Seek the Positive in Life

Even a Watch that Doesn't Work . . .

Seek the Positive in Life

M Y COLLEAGUE, BERNIE, SUFFERED FROM C.B.F. Clergyman's Battle Fatigue. The malady occurs every year at the conclusion of our High Holy Days when congregants conduct a postmortem on the Rabbi's sermons. The critique occurs in Temple parking lots, in the car ride home, in the quiet of suburban homes. Was the sermon too long? Too short? Didn't he use that story last year? Wasn't he really talking about Bobby? You know, in the sermon of a mother who couldn't communicate with her son? What *was* he saying? Why isn't our rabbi more inspirational? More witty? More, more, well, more sermonic. Of course, sometimes the sermons draw rave reviews. "I could have listened to him forever!" (Is this only wishful thinking on my part?)

One year Bernie received especially negative reviews and to unwind joined close friends for dinner after the final service. Somewhere in the middle of the main course, brisket and mashed potatoes, his host, a fervent supporter, commented: "Bernie. Superb. Always superb. The music, beautiful. The special readings, meaningful. And you brought your usual sensitivity to worship. But, I wonder if I could ask one question?"

Bernie's fork froze in the mashed potatoes.

"Why do you always deliver depressing sermons? AIDs, Alzheimer's, Bosnia, the homeless. That's pretty heavy. I come to temple to be uplifted. What can you say that's inspirational?"

Bernie shuddered when he remembered the evening.

"Dan, all I wanted to do was get out of there. Go home. Watch the tennis matches on television. Walk the dog. Anything. I looked at my watch. 4:00. Too early to leave. 4:00? Impossible! Services weren't over until 6:00. It couldn't be 4:00. I tapped the watch. The second hand didn't move. Not only my sermons weren't working. The watch was also broken.

"Then I had a revelation. I remembered a quote I once heard and intended to use when the time was right. 'Even a watch that doesn't work is right twice a day.' Those words would be my save. 4:00. It *had* been 4:00 P.M. It would *be* 4:00 A.M. I turned to my host. 'You want inspiration? Alright. Even a watch that doesn't work is right twice a day.' At first, vacant stares around the table. My host probably thought, Holy Days finally got to the Rabbi. Then I noticed smiles of understanding. I had finally said something upbeat. Even a watch that does not work is right twice a day. All is not lost!"

There are days, even months, when we can not lighten the feeling of gloom that descends upon our lives. We succumb to our despair forgetting even a watch that does not work is right twice a day. These are the times to search for one, maybe two positive thoughts, uplifting events. A sprig of forsythia, a smile, a phone call from a friend, a greeting from a stranger on a neighborhood street will lighten the gloom. Instead of permitting yourself the luxury of self-pity, the feeling that nothing is right with your world, cull the good and every night write in a journal one positive event that occurred that day.

The famous opening line of Charles Dickens' *A Tale of Two Cities* reminds us, "It was the best of times; it was the worst of times." In the worst of times seek the best; life always has a positive component. The watch may be broken, our lives may seem in disarray but we always have the ability to discover, or rediscover, what is right. And if you wish a role model for this attitude permit me to introduce a five-year-old child named Nicholas.

I met Nicholas this summer at a cocktail party hosted by his grandparents in Greenwich, Connecticut. Fifty guests had gathered in early evening, including Nicholas. What does a five year old do among fifty adults? He decided to become a butler. Dressed in a pink polo T-shirt, khaki shorts and docksiders he emerged from the kitchen carrying a silver tray overflowing with egg salad and watercress sandwiches. He stopped near a tall man in a blue blazer. A tall, tall man. Nicholas lifted his head ever so high to see the tall, tall man.

As the child stared, he tilted the silver tray and, one by one the sandwiches slid to the ground. When the majority of the sandwiches had completed their free-fall Nicholas looked down and noticed the disaster. Think. Think for a moment. If this were your child, your grandchild, what would he, or she, have done? Probably drop the tray and run crying into the house.

Not Nicholas. No, this little child with locks of blond hair covering his forehead assessed the damage and with a half smile announced: "Not so bad! Look, four sandwiches survived." Then he added, "I think I'll serve the cookies. They aren't as slippery."

At first I was amazed at this precocious youngster. What five year old would use the word "survived"? Look, four survived! But then I realized Nicholas was blessed with a wisdom far beyond his years. An outlook on life that many of us never achieve.

I intend to chart Nicholas' life. Where will he be twenty years from now? I hope not waiting on tables in New York City! But wherever he may be I am confident he will give thanks for what survives, instead of lamenting what has slipped away—and he will go on.

Life serves up trays filled with joy and with sorrow. Often the joys seem to slip away and we stand empty handed. But not really. Something always remains. A watercress sandwich. An egg salad sandwich. A new friendship. A sunny day. Whatever remains, hold fast and savor those moments that can still provide pleasure and contentment.

Bon Appetit!

Time and Chance Happen to All

Therefore—Appreciate Your Life

T HE UNCERTAINTY OF LIFE. That was the theme of a High Holy Days sermon I wrote one afternoon in mid-September. The uncertainty of life. I had concluded my thoughts with a quote from the biblical book of Ecclesiastes. "I saw under the sun, that the race is not to the swift, nor the battle to the strong, neither yet bread to the wise or riches to men of understanding, but time and chance happen to all."

Satisfied with the sermon I went jogging and, at the end of the driveway, ran into my dog Teddy who had returned from taking my wife Marion for a walk. The three of us talked. (Actually Teddy chased a squirrel but she requested I include her whenever I mention family conversations.) The brief meeting lasted approximately 30 seconds; as you will see, a crucial 30 seconds.

An hour into the jog I passed a pond where ducks splashed playfully. Suddenly, around the bend, I heard a loud cracking sound. Overhead electric wires quivered, went loose, taut, then sagged again. Something was very wrong and I froze in place. The ducks, blessed with wings, soared above an apple orchard and left the scene. Strange thoughts occur at times of potential crisis. I thought about my next life. Not afterlife. Next life when I would return in the form of a duck or an electric wire. Then I went on. Cautiously. Again I heard a sound. The crunch, crunch of brush being trampled. Had a grizzly bear invaded Armonk from the north country? He would not remain. Taxes are too high for even a bear to bear.

Around the bend I observed an electric pole lying across

the blacktop, felled by an ancient maple that had split. When the tree broke, the weight had knocked the pole and the wires onto the ground. I picked my way carefully over the maze of live electric wires and shuddered.

If I had not stopped to talk with Marion and Teddy for 30 seconds, I might have been under those lines.

Stunned, I completed my jog and returned to the holy day sermon. There were the words of Ecclesiastes staring at me from the yellow page. "Time and chance happen to all."

Occasionally I experience flashbacks; picture myself encircled by the limbs of a downed maple tree, the sprawl of electric wires. Words echo. "Dan, no one knows what lies around the bend."

We do not need an electric wire to remind us that our lives are filled with uncertainty. A phone call from a doctor after a routine examination and our life changes. A car skids on a slick road and our life changes. If time and chance happen to all, how should we approach our life?

One alternative is to worry endlessly. A poster reads: "There's a Light at the End of the Tunnel, Lord I Hope It's Not Another Train." A letter begins, "Dear Bob, Start worrying. Details to follow." There are those who live in constant fear; anticipating loss, pain, misfortune. Winston Churchill said, "When I look back on all these worries I remember the story of the old man who said on his deathbed that he had a lot of trouble in his life, most of which never happened." If you must be a worrier, be a discriminating worrier! Compile a list of real worries and imagined worries. The imaginary will far outweigh the real.

Don't worry prematurely! This wisdom was shared with me by an Indian woman I met in the south of India. Her name was Meera and we talked on the porch of a cottage at a retreat called Gravel Banks. Dressed in a tan sari, Meera's gray hair, draped in a single braid, infused the setting with a deep serenity.

We had driven through an endless landscape of tea plantations, broken only by tea pluckers dressed in brightly colored saris with jewelry in their noses, to the tranquil setting outside the Indian village of Munnar. On the porch, surrounded by a moat to fend off wild elephants, I looked out on a pastoral scene, cows crossing a gentle stream.

Meera spoke about a daughter suffering from illness and worried about her future. Hoping to calm the daughter Meera had advised, "We can never know the future, and possibly that is best. It will come. It will come." Now, as we looked upstream at a fisherman lazily casting for trout, Meera sighed. "My child. I try to help her. Coping with suffering is a lonely journey. I know."

With great dignity Meera rose and stood like a statue, her arms folded over her chest. "Sometime ago I was diagnosed with a degenerative eye disease. I went to the specialists in Calcutta, seeking a cure. There is none. Slowly, but irreversibly, I will lose my sight and enter the realm of darkness. All this I told my daughter. She asked, 'Mother how do you face blindness? Perhaps that will help me with my own sickness.'"

"'Child,' I said, 'At first I was afraid but one day, driving to Gravel Banks, I assessed my situation. On the way I had seen a flock of ibex prancing on the rocks, a baby snuggling against its mother. I had marveled at the shades of green painted by nature on the tea leaves. Someday, I realized, I will not see the ibex, or the tea, or delight in the dance of life illumined in my granddaughter's sparkling eyes. Someday. But not yet. I still live in daylight and if I worry about the days after I am blind—then darkness will have already arrived. I will be blind while I can still see.'"

Meera looked at me. "That is what I told my daughter. While there is day why live in fear of night?"

We cannot know what lies around the bend or when night may approach, but restrain your fears. John Milton wrote, "The mind is its own place, and in itself can make a heaven of hell or a hell of heaven." Hold a stop sign before your imagination, conjure up a red light the moment you find your mind drifting to the "what might happens." "What might happen if the doctor's report is positive?" "What might happen if the plane crashes?" "What might happen if the scenario I orchestrated for myself fails?" Imagine a red light, a stop sign. Then, when you have stopped the mind from racing furiously, conjure up an image that brings joy. A child's smile. Waters off the coast of Maine. The flowing maple trees of autumn. Life has bright moments. Life has dark moments. Happiness consists of choosing which hours to dwell upon.

Another suggestion. When you are afraid, calm yourself by conceiving of fear as an invisible veil. Walk through the veil. Skaters, when they come to thin ice, do not stop. To stop increases the chance of breaking through. Glide forward until you move beyond the danger—real or anticipated.

A remarkable example of the ability to move beyond fear was exhibited by a woman I met while hiking in the Himalayas. Her words began: "In Dachau I did not know if I would live until the next morning."

I was sitting with Greta beneath the black peak of Mount Everest. Greta seemed ill-suited for trekking at fourteen thousand feet in the Himalayan Mountains but with the aid of a Sherpa guide she struggled into camp each afternoon as the sun tucked itself behind a mountain ridge. She apologized for always falling behind. "I had open-heart surgery last year, when I turned seventy-one. Sometimes my breath is short at these altitudes."

"Aren't you afraid?" I asked. "We're six days from civilization. What if something happens? Why did you come to Nepal?"

Greta smiled, the smile of one who has entered worlds I will never understand.

"When I was sixty-two, the year my husband died, I made my first sky dive over Lake Annecy. My friends thought I had a death wish. They thought I had guilt that I had survived the Holocaust and that was why I courted danger. I told them I had a life wish. In the winter of 1943 I was only a number; huddled among children in the concentration camp at Dachau; fighting for a chunk of moldy bread. I survived and came through that experience with my spirit intact. When I was liberated I promised myself not to live out my days in fear—especially of events I am powerless to control.

"Why do I hike at fourteen thousand feet? Because if I ever surrender to fear I surrender life."

Time and chance do happen to all but they need not diminish our lives. Uncertainty seldom looms as high as a mountain in Nepal. It is not as dark as blindness. What lies around the bend? No one knows, but on the journey encourage your hopes, not your fears.

The Caper Phenomenon

Come Back from Adversity

O NLY A CAPER PLANT MARRED the finely cultivated garden of
the French Consulate on Rue Paul Emil Botta Street. The
bushy tentacles, green buds slowly opening into a pink
flower, prodded the unwary passerby as the plant pushed its way
out of the sun-bleached stone wall surrounding the consulate.

I stood in the garden, dwarfed by the massive grey stone of
the Old City of Jerusalem and imagined Israelites, Romans,
Crusaders, and Ottomans who had lingered at this site. Today
only a Moroccan gardener, carefully pruning the bushes, occupied
the grounds. When he rested on a bench I asked the swarthy man,
"Why don't you trim back the caper? It's the only wild plant in the
garden. It doesn't belong here. Can't you do something?"

The gardener pointed at the caper with his pruning shears.
"Sir, do you know the caper?" I shook my head. He explained.
"When I first came to work at the consulate I asked the same question of my Yemenite boss. 'Why don't you trim back the caper?' He
grinned. 'Jacques, cut back the caper if you wish. See what happens.' Well, I did—back to the surface of the stone. For several days
not a trace of the plant. Then, out of the crack in the stone the caper
came back. The pink stems. Again I cut. Again the stems grew,
stronger than before. Finally I made peace with the caper."

Holding up a thorny branch he looked with admiration at the
plant whose branches draped over the wall. "You cannot kill the

caper. Each time you cut them back they return. With more force. I have seen them split sidewalks in two. If they have the slightest breath of air, the smallest crack, they push their way into life. The caper never gives up. Against all odds. How can you help but admire the plant's desire to live? How? Maybe more of us should follow the caper."

And the wiry old man returned to his gardening.

After that day in Jerusalem I became an advocate of the Caper Phenomenon; an ability to seize upon the slightest opportunity and push forward in life. At one time or another each of us experiences a period when our days seem too heavy to bear; when the life-giving forces of laughter, love, contentment evaporate and are cut away at the roots. Where do we find the inspiration to come back? From within. The Caper Phenomenon assumes we are more self-sufficient than we might acknowledge. No one fertilizes the caper. No one waters this stubborn plant, but somehow the caper draws upon inner resources.

For decades I have watched *The Wizard of Oz*, through my childhood and through my children's years. Every time the lovable lion strolls along the yellow brick road in his quest for courage I join the procession. Maybe this will be the year the wizard grants courage to the lion. And every year, as we meet in the Emerald City of Oz, I realize once again that the wizard cannot give courage. The wizard cannot give what the lion does not already have. When the lion searches inside his own soul (assuming lions have souls!) he discovers courage.

We all have more inner resources than we acknowledge. To nurture the Caper Phenomenon remind yourself of a moment when you said: "I can't go on," but you did. Realize that everyone has at least one spark that can be kindled and a single spark may effectively light our way. Albert Schweitzer taught, "We see not power in a drop of water. But let it get into a crack in the rock and be turned to ice and it splits the rock; turned into steam it drives the pistons of the most powerful engines. Something has happened to it which makes active the power that is latent in it." One good thought, one glimmer of hope can blossom forth into a new day. The poet Langston Hughes asked, "What happens to a dream deferred? Does it dry up like a raisin in the sun?" The choice is yours. Once you accept the premise that, like the caper, you can come back, then dreams take on a life of their own.

A spouse dies. A loved one. The family worries. "How will my father continue? Mother took care of him." But, to the surprise of everyone, the survivor finds a new partner. Does this mean he did not deeply love his first wife? Of course not. It means that if we have the power to love we can love over and over again. This is the regenerative nature of the Caper Phenomenon. Each of us is a complex assortment of many rooms, diverse compartments. When one door closes locate another door, like the caper tracking an opening beneath soil.

Of the many people who demonstrate the Caper Phenomenon one of the most impressive examples was Lore, a Holocaust survivor. We stood in the art gallery at our temple.

"I was only a child when the Nazis came for us," Lore reminisced. "It was on the Sabbath. At dinner. My father had made the blessing over the wine. We heard a knock in our house off the Grabestrasse. Next to the canal. Who would knock on the Sabbath? I think my father knew without opening the door. We had lived in fear of that knock, hoping it would never come. But my father knew the Gestapo. Before we were herded into the ghetto, my father went from room to room in our brownstone turning off the lights. The Nazi's prodded us to hurry and my father turned off the lights. I will never forget that gesture of defiance; his footsteps echoed on the wooden floorboards as he turned off the lights, before the darkness of the concentration camps engulfed us."

Lore stopped, breathing heavily from the pain of recollection.

"The rest you know," she continued as her chest heaved. "The rest you know. Or you have read. I was sent to Theriesenstadt; my parents to their death. Like most survivors, I am still haunted by the Holocaust in dreams at night, when I hear sirens on the streets, when I see tattoos; not tattoos from the camps but tattoos the young place on their bodies today. A butterfly, a scorpion, even a heart burned into a shoulder. Before they brand themselves they should come to me. I will tell them how a body may be disfigured."

Suddenly Lore's mood changed, her eyes brightened. "Dan, when I dwell on the Holocaust I also remember the incredible courage. We were powerless to stop Hitler but in a thousand small ways the victims demonstrated they would not be defeated. A rabbi secretly conducting services in a barracks at Auschwitz; a mother singing a lullaby to her child; a boy offering his meal, a plateful of moldy potatoes, to an old man. And those who survived, they began again. Neighbors from my hometown in Holland lost everyone, remarried, started life over. They rose out of the depths of despair. 'Out of the depths I call to you Oh Lord. Answer me.' Beyond the atrocities I remember the indomitable will. That's what I remember."

I stared out of the large glass windows of the art gallery unable to speak, silenced by the faith of this woman who, in spite of everything, could still believe—if not in the goodness of humanity—in the resurgent strength of people. Then she saw it, a yellow crocus blooming in the February sun and surrounded by snow. Her face beamed. "See, Dan, a crocus. My favorite flower. It has no business blooming in February. Next week we'll have a snowfall and the flower will be buried. But that crocus will come back, if not this year, next. Given a few days of warmth and the crocus wants to explore life. Incredible."

"I think I understand your love of the crocus," I said softly. "For you the crocus represents the power to be reborn, to seek a new springtime, no matter what the odds."

Lore nodded. "The French philosopher Albert Camus wrote, 'In the midst of winter I finally learned that there was within me an invincible summer.' I have borne witness to that invincible summer, that seed of hope. I have borne witness."

Those of us who did not walk the chambers of the Holocaust can never grasp the enormity of that horror. But anyone on a winter's day can witness a crocus struggling to emerge. Anyone can look beneath the snow to find spring in preparation under the blanket of winter. Whenever we encounter defeat and find the strength to burst out from the bonds we come back stronger. Scars remain but scar tissue is the strongest tissue.

We cannot purge life of sorrow but we can triumph over that sorrow. The caper says: "Cut me back. Sever my branches, but I will reemerge on another day."

We may learn from the caper.

Run a Marathon

Life Goes On

WHY RUN THE MARATHON?

The sense of accomplishment? The runners high? The opportunity to gorge yourself with pasta the night before?

For Dr. Tim Cleary, sprawled on the grass in Central Park after completing his first marathon in a time he begged me not to quote, "You can tell my story but not my time," the race concluded a poignant drama. I had happened upon the final chapter of a promise.

I met Tim Cleary a decade earlier in Jerusalem, before his goatee had turned white and his stomach draped over baggy shorts. At that time he was on sabbatical from teaching philosophy at a small college in central Illinois. He missed his wife Peg, "especially our early morning jog through cornfields. You can run forever and never run out of cornfields!"

In the prime of health he and Peg had written ethical wills. "We instructed our children not to take unnecessary measures to prolong our life. We did not want to go on as vegetables. 'Richness of life,' we told the kids, 'Not number of days.' I was ready to sign the document and send it off to the lawyer but Peg, with a twinkle in her eyes, said:

"Not so fast Tim. I want to make a pact."

"I should explain," Tim went on, "Peg teaches romance literature. I envisioned the pact of a balding midwestern professor and
his wife hurling themselves off a cliff at the edge of a cornfield;
hand in hand, tumbling to their death."

Peg had another thought in mind.

"Tim, whoever dies first, the surviving partner promises to
run the New York Marathon."

"A marathon? We have enough trouble stumbling through
six miles. A marathon?"

"Peg was insistent. 'It's just a matter of training. Training.'"

"You've lost me," I told Peg. "Why would I want to run a
marathon if you died?"

"To prove that life has a start. Life has an end. But the race
begins all over again. That's why. And to prove that we can go on.
Without each other."

Tim laughed. "I agreed. Assuming we would live into our
nineties, memories failing, who would remember the pact?"

After that conversation with Tim I occasionally saw him in
Jerusalem.

"How's Peg?" I would ask.

"Fine, fine."

I knew Tim had yet to run the marathon—until that day in
Central Park when Tim crawled out from under a silver space
blanket. All I could say was, "I'm sorry." That's when Tim smiled
and said, "You can tell my story but not my time. It was too long."
He fought back tears. "No, Dan it was too short." The tears
flowed. "Peg died of breast cancer last December. That's why I
wasn't in Jerusalem over the summer. But I kept my promise. I ran
the marathon."

I was silent. What could I say to this man? Sadness etched a
path from his silver sideburns to his quivering lips, but I knew he
would pull through. Even without Peg. Tim would be fine.

How do we recover from loss? Most of us would not elect to
run a marathon, but every step we take helps us to reenter the
world. No one can take that step for you. No one can help you

begin again after the loss of a loved one, a dream, or something as basic as a job. Everyone finds their own approach to ease the way back. Often it is a solitary and lonely procedure.

Years ago my Aunt Teresa lost her son in the Korean War. Weeks later her husband died of a heart attack. I visited Aunt Teresa in Minneapolis hoping to fill a small segment of her emptiness, but instead of discovering a woman whose life had stopped I found a person overly programmed. A visit from medical school students in early morning, weeding the garden, a luncheon appointment, bridge. The list stretched on and on. After several days of activities I looked at Aunt Teresa. "You're very fortunate to have so many interests." She smiled "Interests? These are time fillers to see me through the day. At night I make a list for the following day." Months later I returned to Minneapolis. The lists had vanished. "Now I only do what gives me satisfaction." She had reentered life.

George Bernard Shaw wrote. "People are always blaming their circumstances for what they are. I don't believe in circumstances. The people who get on in the world are the people who get up and look for the circumstances they want, and, if they can't find them, make them." Teresa responded to difficult circumstances by shaping her life in a new way. At first the imprint was artificial but gradually events took on a reality and the joy of living returned.

When I visit Jerusalem I spend time with a lovely woman in her rooftop garden overlooking the Western Wall. Miriam lost her son to an artillery shell in one of Israel's wars. On early visits Miriam succumbed to her loss but one year she pointed to a shell in the far corner of her rooftop garden; an artillery shell. Similar to the one that had killed Rafi. Dirt spilled out of the shell and in that dirt Miriam had planted a vine; yellow flowers cascaded down the sides. Miriam had planted life in a symbol of death. It was her way of coming back.

Have you lost a loved one? Travel on new roads with new acquaintances. No one will replace the one you loved, but there are many people who can give satisfaction in different and exciting ways. When children have left for college, children in whose life you have been entwined, fulfill your own postponed dreams. This is your time. If a change has been forced upon your career, not through any choice of your own, immediately begin to seek new avenues of employment. Investigate diverse areas until you have reestablished your focus. There are times in our lives when the key is not the goal but the process of beginning again. We constantly reinvent our lives.Oliver Wendell Holmes commented, "It is not as important where we stand as in what direction we are moving."

We are never at the finish line.

A Case for Tunnel Vision

Encounter the Unpleasant

S INCE I WAS A CHILD I HAVE avoided tunnels. Why? From claustrophobia, the irrational fear that someday I will enter a tunnel without an exit? Because of a bad experience when I was a baby? Whatever the reason, I will explore every byway, pursue every path to reach my destination without passing through a tunnel.

Therefore, I shuddered when the car rental agent at the airport in Marseilles informed me, "You wish to drive to Cassis? Très charming. Only forty-five minutes from here. Along the seashore. Just take the peage to the tunnel one kilometer from Marseilles."

Those words. "The tunnel."

"Excuse me," I asked in my most charming American accent. "Can I avoid the tunnel?" She laughed. "No, no, Monsieur, the tunnel to Cassis" and, handing me the keys to the Citroen, she took her lunch break. Leaving the airport I watched for the sign to Marseilles. Aix en Provence, Toulon, Avignon, Aubague but not a sign to Marseilles. How could I be lost before I even began? My wife, Marion, reminded me that in my case this was an easy feat. We stopped at a gas station to ask for the road to Marseilles and were informed we were on the road. "That is why there are no signs." For once I had actually driven in the right direction. I apologized to Marion and promised this would never happen again.

Ten minutes later I whizzed onto the peage. Supremely confident I even passed a 1960s Peugeot driven by an elderly French couple who seemed better suited to driving in Florida than on the speedways of Europe. A huge green sign zoomed overhead; the word TUNNEL flashed in white lights. No one could miss this sign. No one could miss this tunnel. I did. At least that's how Marion tells the story. Actually I was in the far right lane, unable to cut over to the left, the tunnel lane, without an intimate encounter with a Mercedes, a Renault, and an interstate truck.

That is how I missed the tunnel and found myself in the middle of Marseilles, where guide books warned, "Do not drive into Marseilles. Take a train." At least we were following the coast in the direction of Cassis. "This is a better way Marion, and I can avoid the tunnel." Unfortunately, the road ended at a seaside cliff where I made a U-turn, attracting a chorus of horns and successfully cutting off a Porsche, which normally would have been a sufficient accomplishment for one day. Now we were back in our original direction. "Marion, I'm going to go right here. Maybe we'll find another road. A shortcut to Cassis."

Marion grimaced. "If you go right you will be in the Mediterranean," which was only partially correct. The right turn took me out on a long jetty but, please believe me, I never went into the water. Marion urged me to find the sign TUNNEL but, still resistant, I followed a quiet tree-lined boulevard into a parking lot.

In biblical times a prophet named Jonah, also hanging out on the Mediterranean coast, lost his way and blundered into the stomach of a whale. After three days he called out, "God, get me out of here. I'll do whatever you want" (loose translation). After 30 minutes of Marseilles, bouillabaisse capital of the world, I also called: "God, get me out of here. I'm ready to try the tunnel." God heard my supplication and I spied that familiar green sign, TUNNEL. Marion pleaded, "Dan, this time pay attention. Please."

I did. After three minutes of darkness we exited on the sun bathed road to Cassis.

In retrospect, the tunnel experience, although not pleasant, proved relatively easy; at least it was easier than trying to avoid the inevitable. I understood the car rental agent's words, "Find the tunnel." There are times when we cannot avoid tunnels, dark moments when we feel the world closing in on us, problems looming before us. At such times we would like to flee, find a detour or a shortcut. One may not exist. Our only option? To confront what lies ahead. TUNNEL. The sooner we enter, the sooner we exit, onto a road bright with sunshine.

Eleanor Roosevelt said: "You gain strength, courage, and confidence by every experience in which you really stop to look fear in the face. You are able to say to yourself, I lived through this horror. I can take the next thing that comes along."

When was the last time you looked fear in the face and moved through the obstacles that lay ahead? Close your eyes. Imagine a tunnel. The darkness. Imagine yourself groping on the way. Then imagine a glimmer of sunlight at the far end. Brighter. Brighter. You are on the road to Cassis. And traversing the first tunnel eases the journey through tunnels to follow.

Most of us avoid what we find unpleasant. Perhaps, we reason, if we close our eyes difficulties will disappear. Instead they gnaw at our inner fiber. The story is told of a man who has lost his car keys late at night and searches by the side of the road. A second man approaches and hoping to be helpful asks,

"Where did you lose the keys?"

"On the other side of the road."

"Then why are you searching here?"

"Because this is where the light is."

But where the light is may not be where we find the key to our problem. We may need to search in the darkness—at least for awhile. When I was growing up, a Saturday ritual in Albany, New York involved the movies at the Madison Avenue Theater. Preceding the feature presentation we were treated to a serial starring The Lone Ranger. Week after week The Lone Ranger would be poised in some precarious position and, at some spine tingling moment, the installment ended. There he was, hanging onto the edge of a cliff pursued by villains. Would The Lone Ranger leap the chasm? Would he reach the far side? Come back in a week. For seven days I anticipated the next chapter of The Lone Ranger's adventures. Now, with the maturity of the years, I understand my waiting was insignificant compared to The Lone Ranger's.

Hanging onto the edge of a cliff for seven days.

What do you think The Lone Ranger did for those seven days while I went back to school? I imagine he yelled: "Put the film on fast forward! Don't leave me hanging! Let me jump! Please, I want to jump to the other side!"

We cannot put our lives on fast forward but we do not need to stop the reel by refusing to jump; by postponing what we dread but have to face.

Avoidance has existed since earliest time. For instance, one of the biblical heroes was a man named Jacob. In his youth Jacob was not an All Hebrew role model. He stole his brother's birthright, deceived Isaac his father, and ran away from home. Hardly an auspicious beginning. Finally, after twenty-one years, Jacob once again encountered his brother Esau in a barren wilderness. Should he run? Find another route and evade his brother? Avoid his past? Not this time. Fearfully Jacob faced Esau and the brothers reconciled. Although not there to read Jacob's mind when he and Esau embraced, I assume Jacob wondered: "Why did I wait twenty-one years? Why did I run for twenty-one years? If I had faced Esau years ago I may have been able to return to the security of home." Jacob had entered his tunnel. In the future he could travel on brighter roads. Finally, Jacob could become a biblical hero.

Entering a tunnel takes more than an accurate sense of direction. It implies the courage to meet what we dread. The way is through, not around.

That is why I make this case for tunnel vision.

Rocky I, II, III, IV

Accept Reality. Problems Never Cease

I TOLD MY NEIGHBOR BURT HE SHOULD write the authoritative book on gardening and the art of living. Burt initiated me into the joys and travails of gardening when I moved into my house on Tripp Street. I envied his zucchini (the size of baseball bats), raspberry bushes (luxuriant with deep red berries), rows of tomatoes (pulled earthward by their heavy fruit).

I decided to be a farmer. With Burt's assistance we researched seed catalogs from Burpee to Vermont Bean and, by late spring, I had gained control of the seed market. If all these seeds grew I could become a major supplier to the Hunts Point Market, a force to be dealt with. Actually my goals were modest: dig a few holes, pop in a few seeds, sit back, and pick. But Burt, my good gardening conscience, warned: "Not so fast, Dan. First we have to turn over the ground, then put up a fence to keep out animals" . . . the litany continued. "Of course, that's if you want a good garden. Up to you."

Reluctantly I agreed and waited until the morning I heard Burt's tractor snorting, growling, and chugging from his yard to mine. The tractor, determined to conquer packed earth untouched for seventy years, gnawed away at the ground, its iron teeth biting into a mix of rock and earth. At midday Burt still battled the soil, until a distraught Marion appeared. My wife complained,

"Another disaster!" I reminded her I had not had a disaster for almost a year—not since the time I painted the picket fence three shades of white.

The next morning, clutching my basket of seeds, I raced out to the garden but Burt's voice floated over from the deck. "Not so fast, Dan. Not so fast." Leaning against the fence I stared at Burt. "What's wrong?"

"I turned over the ground but you have to clear the stones. This is old Yankee ground. Tenth generation rocks. Your young plants won't stand a chance." So I cleared rocks. For three days I cleared rocks. Up, down. Up, down. Into the wheelbarrow. When I eventually sowed my garden I grew a crop of vegetables worthy of a veteran farmer.

Over the winter I relaxed and thought, next spring planting will be easy, but when Burt turned over the soil I discovered last year's stones had returned. I accused Burt of delivering my old stones. He laughed. "They look like last year's but they're different." Then, crawling under the tractor to repair an axle split by a rock, he shared a seed of Yankee wisdom. "Rain, spring thaw, the ground settles. Rocks reappear. That's the way it is; clear out the stones one year, seems okay for awhile, then another pile appears." Peeking out from under the tail pipe he added, "Isn't that the way it is with life, Dan? Clear out one set of problems, another rears its head."

I shrugged.

"So what can I do, Burt?"

"Start carting."

I have. Every year. I don't mind; neither does my local pharmacist who supplies me with muscle relaxants, and greets me with the question: "Still carting, Dan?" I answer, "Yes."

Koheleth, author of the biblical book of Ecclesiastes, philosophized, "To everything there is a season and a time to every purpose under the heaven . . . a time to cast away stones and a time to gather stones together." Koheleth understood the cyclical aspect of life, even in the realm of stones.

We never cast away all the stones that bruise the fabric of our lives. We may hope for permanent answers, for a clear playing field on which to maneuver, but obstacles always arise. Some new. Some old.

Instead of wishing for a garden free of stones, learn how to clear those stones. Everyone has some weight that makes life more difficult. The secret lies not in being free of burdens but in our ability to carry those burdens. Never envy another person. Life scatters obstacles indiscriminately. Envy those who can navigate the years with these obstacles. When working with cancer patients I am impressed by patients who, flung back time and time again, never succumb; these exceptional individuals constantly hold out for another treatment, a cure still undiscovered, a miracle. In his latter years, Booker T. Washington wrote, "I have learned that success is to be measured not so much by the position that one has reached in life as by the obstacles which he has overcome when trying to succeed."

Take life's hardships in their time. Clear one stone and then another. Rake the leaves on Wednesday, watch them blow back on Friday—but enjoy Thursday. Think of the satisfaction you can gain each time you remove a stumbling block from the way.

In the essay "The Myth of Sisyphus" Albert Camus writes:

> *The Gods had condemned Sisyphus to ceaselessly rolling a rock to the top of a mountain, whence the stone would fall back of its own weigh. . . . I see that man, going back down with a heavy yet measured step toward the torment of which he will never know the end. At each of those moments when he leaves the heights and gradually sinks toward the lairs of the gods, he is superior to his fate. He is stronger than his rock. The struggle itself toward the height is enough to fill a man's heart. One must imagine Sisyphus happy.*

Each one of us carries the weight, the burdens of private lands we can never conquer, distant vistas towards which we move and never reach, but it is only when we cease trying, cease growing, that we are defeated.

Conceive of life as on ageless process of clearing, sowing, clearing, sowing. And take satisfaction in every season.

A Tribute to the Yellow Pad

Correct Your Life

I AM A FOSSIL! WHAT CONFIRMS THIS self-evaluation? Not one word of this book was written on a computer! It is 1998 and I am computer illiterate. Everyone uses a computer! Even children feel comfortable with Macs, PCs, dissing and dossing. As a clergyman by profession I spend my days surfing in the heavenly realm, searching for some revelation while the seven-year-old son of my secretary surfs the Internet. In fact, not long ago, Johnny, a first grader from my religious school, came into my study with a laptop computer in his pink schoolbag. Rising to his full height of three feet, six inches, he explained that he was an emissary (not his word) from the first grade. Then he read a computer printout. "Dear Rabbi, the first grade will not believe in God unless you believe in a computer." To keep my young friend on his toes I explained that God created the entire world without an IBM or a Mac. Startled, Johnny cried out, "That's a miracle!"

Why do I resist the computer age? Because of personal resentment? A bad childhood experience? A fixation on the past? None of the above. I shun computers because I love yellow pads. This book was written on a yellow pad. There. It's out. I love yellow pads! I feel better confessing my love of yellow pads. How could I ever create without a yellow pad? When I sit at my desk, surrounded by stack upon stack of yellow pads, I feel a security certain psychiatrists have labeled YPS. Yellow Pad Syndrome. That is why I do not use a computer. That is why I risk turning the first grade into a class of nonbelievers. That is why I am a fossil.

I am proud that in a world too often devoid of principle I have not yet been computer programmed. Whenever possible I continue to fight the good fight. The yellow pad fight. For instance, I am in negotiation with my publisher to insert two sheets of yellow lined paper in every copy of this book. This singular action would describe my personality far better than the brief autobiography on the jacket: "Daniel Wolk lives in Mount Kisco, New York with his wife Marion, dog Teddy, eighteen deer, five woodchucks, thirty-seven chipmunks, and so on, and so on." And I am pleased to announce that in the forty-seventh printing, or after I sell one million books, whichever comes first, yellow pages *will* accompany each book. I trust word of mouth will turn my dream into a reality and I will reach this modest sales figure.

At this time you, the reader, have every reason to inquire: "Why the devotion to a yellow pad?" I will explain with a real life experience when Saul, the temple's computer wizard, asked me to join him for a new demonstration of software acquired by our office.

"Ten minutes, Dan, that's all I need."

Cautiously I ambled over to the computer. I was familiar with these tactics, used by cults all over the world. "A few moments, sir. Just listen for a few minutes. You desire peace? Contentment? Come closer." The next thing you know they've swept you off the street and plunked you in some isolated room and you're lost. Lost to the world. Would Saul snatch me off the office floor and lock me in the storeroom of Nobody Beats The Wiz, where I would succumb to the nefarious Computer Cult?

Slowly the green screen flashed and Saul fiddled with the keyboard. The words "Hi, Dan, don't be afraid, I offer salvation," appeared on the screen. I retreated. "Wait, Dan. Just kidding about the salvation thing. Wanted to reach a common ground. Read this!" The computer quickly made its case for why I should forsake yellow pads. "Ten Commandments for Changing to Computers."

1. Thou shalt have no other gods before me.
2. Honor your hard drive and soft drive
3. Remember the computer way and keep it holy
4. Thou shalt not kill unnecessary paper
5. Thou shalt not commit upholstery (the computer knew the upholstery on the chair where I wrote was filled with ink stains)
6. Thou shalt not covet thy neighbor's wife, nor his ass, nor his yellow pad.

And so on, and so on, and so on.

Forsaking the Ten Commandments, the computer honed in on its most convincing argument.

"I will help you edit. Dissatisfied with a word, a sentence, a paragraph? Erase me! Pretend I never existed. Forget the messy task of crossing out, scrawling in margins, placing arrows here, there, and everywhere. Press delete. Vavoom! Gone! A clean screen!"

Then, seductively, the computer wrote, "Come closer, Dan, touch me. Feel my smooth lines, my floppy disc, my. . . ."

I bolted into my office, apologized to a waiting yellow pad for flirting with a computer and scribbled a reply to the green screen.

Dear R-Rated Computer,
I do not intend to comment on your outrageous show of sexual harassment or your simplistic rendering of the Ten Commandments; although permit me to mention that if Moses had any inkling (*I intentionally inserted "ink" to aggravate the computer*). . . . If Moses had any inkling that he would inscribe tablets with *your* Ten Commandments he would not have wasted forty days on Mount Sinai!

But let me discuss the core of your argument. As a computer you contain the power to erase what you do not like. That may work for a computer but not in real life. Off the screen we live with our errors, regrets, mistakes. The past leaves an indelible mark. Good and bad. When I scan my yellow sheets I understand what worked, what did not work. I learn from the crossed out portions and move forward onto the blank pages of hope.

In brief, I believe life consists of corrections not erasures.

~~With best wishes~~

Sincerely,

Dan

Have you ever said to yourself: "If only I could begin again," "Why, why did I say that to my daughter-in-law, wife, son, boss." Fill in the blanks. "Give me another chance. Wipe the slate clean. Next time I will do it right. Please. . . ." Sorry. Life seldom offers a clean slate, but we are granted the opportunity to correct our mistakes and move on

When you make a mistake, (and who does not occasionally make a mistake?) do you proceed from that point, or, discouraged, do you give up? At my temple we have a custodian, Enrique, who was blessed with the ability to fix any appliance—even toasters programmed to break down after a year's use. Enrique is anathema in today's throw away world and his storeroom spills over with my household goods. Before Enrique came on the scene I threw away lamps, Walkmans, and, of course, toasters when they broke. After all, isn't that the patriotic American way? Enrique rescued one especially stubborn portable fan from the trash and promised me that in a week it would be "good as new," which I believed to be a lot of hot air. Actually I did not want him to fix the fan. I had my eye on a new Super 3-Speed that I didn't need. On the day of my planned purchase, before I could escape in my Toyota, (which is also breaking down), Enrique appeared with the restored fan.

In contrast to Enrique, I come from a noncorrective family. For instance, last summer my fiberglass canoe, an old war horse that had weathered intimate encounters with every rock in Brant Lake, developed severe arthritis and broke in half. This was the opportunity my wife and sons had awaited for many years. "Get rid of that old canoe, Dan. It's an embarrassment on the lake. A sordid orange body covered with mud colored patches. Time for a new spiffy Kevlar canoe!"

I made a pilgrimage to a local craftsman whose canoes had earned him a reputation in the Adirondacks. My family's eyes sparkled when the canoe maker unveiled a sleek 28 pound hunter green beauty. Sadly I dipped my paddle in the water. "What's wrong?," someone asked and I blurted out the truth: "I don't want to abandon my old canoe!" The canoe maker asked "What happened to the canoe?" I explained the slight problem. "The front separated from the back!" To my amazement this seller of $1,700 canoes came up with a proposal. "I can fix your old canoe. Probably cost about $30." Happy ending! What a wonderful man! Now I paddle (alone) in my orange canoe, a living witness to the fact that life can be fixed.

Enrique, the canoe manufacturer, and I belong to the school of thought that believes we can correct our lives. When deprived of the ability to start again, when the part cannot be erased, find a patch, offer an apology, change direction, add or subtract an element of your life.

I would be interested in knowing what you have corrected lately. What needs to be corrected? Please send me your list on a sheet from a yellow pad.

Why Should Your Control Be Remote

Simplify Your Problems

WHO COULD I BLAME? There I was, standing in the rain in the dark of night, unable to open my garage door. Who could I blame when I forgot the code on the pad fixed to the side of the garage? I had never used the code. I had my remote control, but the remote control failed to open the garage door. Who could I blame?

I had warning. For three weeks the garage door hesitated before opening. Cranky, I thought. Then, the opener staged a partial shutdown. Monday? Yes. Tuesday? No. Sometimes the door opened half way and I crawled under; or honked for my wife. Tonight? Nothing. Who could I blame?

Who? Who? Who? Oh! That horrible feeling of wanting someone to blame, but not a soul volunteered! I'd start with God. The Industrial Revolution. Poor choices. They were nowhere to be found. Who could I blame? I was becoming desperate. Mosner's Appliance! That's it, Mosner's Appliance where I bought the remote control. Brandishing my remote like a warrior's club I charged through the store door and zapped Ms. O'Dwyer, the polite receptionist. At first nothing opened. Then her mouth opened slightly and an insidious word escaped from between her lips. "Yes?" The way she said it. I knew. Ms. O'Dwyer was in league with this remote control, with all remote controls. I wouldn't fall for the ruse.

"I demand to see the manager!" I yelled, pointing my remote control at every television set in the store. I was out of control, even remote control. Ms. O'Dwyer tried to calm me but she had already pushed my buttons with that one word, "Yes?"

"Sir," she said calmly. Oh! Whoever programmed that woman did a masterful job. "Doug's out now, installing a garage door opener. Can I help?"

"You! How can you help! I need a technician, an electrician, a computer whiz. My garage door opener won't work." Speaking slowly and distinctly to emphasize the gravity of my problem I insisted: "I need Doug."

"Please," the receptionist said gently, "Please let me look at the control."

Reluctantly I handed over the dastardly appliance. She tinkered with the black box, disappeared into the workshop and reemerged with a 9-volt battery. "Your battery was dead. Try it now." After threatening Ms. O'Dwyer with consumer fraud if the opener did not work I returned home. Before I reached the driveway I pushed the button. Cheerfully the door rose.

Later I called Ms. O'Dwyer to apologize. "I may have overreacted." Adding, "Slightly."

Her voice echoed at the other end of the phone. "Sometimes I'm under stress in my home also."

"But this was outside my house," I insisted.

Aware of her customer's penchant for sudden anger Mrs. O'Dwyer purred: "Sometimes all you really need is a little thing like a battery."

Ms. O'Dwyer, you chose the wrong profession. You should be writing these stories, tacking a little moral on the end. How did you know answers may be as elementary as changing a battery? We rant. We rave. We shiver in a cold rain. We avoid confronting our problems. Or place obstacles where there are none. Often the answer is quite simple.

How did Ms. O'Dwyer fix my remote control? With a new battery? Only partially. Her true genius lay in her ability to take a problem, analyze the pieces and not overreact. In our high-stress society, lives as well as technology often break down. Instead of allowing a problem to get out of hand, evaluate the situation, and instead of assuming the worst, begin with the known.

When was the last time a situation escalated out of control? Was the answer really that complex? When did an aspirin or a good night's sleep cure an illness you thought might be terminal? Begin with the obvious before yelling "May-day! May-day!" Accept the possibility that perhaps you can solve the dilemma instead of barging into Mosner's Appliance Store.

Years ago I read a book by Hugh Walpole entitled *Fortitude*. I have long since forgotten the story except for a vivid image at the beginning and end. A boy enters a town in England and notices a stone lion in the square. Suddenly the boy imagines the lion is riding him to some unknown destination. At the conclusion of the book the boy returns to the square. This time he is riding the lion. What happened in between? The hero gained mastery over his life.

Our lives are not really out of control unless we relinquish our own ability to shape their form. Often we complicate life, make our problems too complex instead of breaking them into solvable elements. Like a battery.

Why are we Eveready to make life more difficult than necessary? Only you can answer that question.

The Mender of Cracked Pots

Put the Pieces of Life Together

N ILA WORKED WITH CRACKED POTS while sitting at a table under a eucalyptus tree. These were not the cracked pots of contemporary vernacular. Nila was an archeological restorer at the site of the biblical town of Dan, once the northernmost border of the land of Israel and the pottery in front of her dated to the year 1000 B.C.E.

One pot, slowly emerging from the artist's hands, captivated me. A day earlier I excavated this jug with the swing of a pick ax and heard the resonant sound of metal against pottery! I carefully removed remnants of a tall elliptical jug used to store spices. After dusting off the shards I brought them to Nila thinking, "Well, jar, after three thousand years of burial you've been reborn. There is hope for all who wait."

In the course of the week I admired Nila's handiwork. She would hunt for matching pot shards and tape them together before applying a permanent adhesive. I wondered wistfully what she would charge to come to Mount Kisco and complete the jigsaw puzzle sprawled over my dining room table. No one in our family wished to dismantle the puzzle but no one could finish the design, "White on White." Nila would redeem the walnut table; perhaps even free the surface for dinner!

As I watched the jar take shape, my mind journeyed to the

distant past, three thousand years ago. A camel caravan appeared on the horizon, camel bags filled with myrrh and frankincense. Since my name was Dan I was selected by the elders of the town of Dan to bargain with the tribal chieftain. After settling on a price, the precious myrrh was poured into my jug until the rounded top overflowed.

I returned to the present and looked out toward the horizon, searching for camels swaying in burned-out fields. A cow sauntered down a path and my reverie of spice trading faded across the Lebanese border. The jug would not meet a mysterious caravan; rather, the pottery, packed into the rear of a jeep, would be sent to Jerusalem for display at the Israel Museum.

Gradually Nila completed her work. The majority of remnants had been retrieved, but some would remain buried for eternity. Nila filled the empty spaces with molded clumps of red clay. Finally, the jug stood proudly on the table, dwarfing a pilgrim's flask (the ancient prototype of a canteen) and a four-spouted pottery oil lamp. Another chapter in the history of Dan, visited by the patriarch Abraham, governed by kings with the names of Jeroboam and Reheboam, had come to life.

I stepped back to admire the jar and complimented Nila on her artistry. Cracks zigzagged over the surface where jagged edges came together. Nila smiled as she peeled glue off of her hands. "Not perfect, but the best I could do with what I had." What had Nila done? She had taken the pieces available to her and molded a jar that could, if necessary, hold spices.

As I watched the artist I imagined her putting together the remnants of life. Life overflows with broken dreams, love shattered by divorce, death, loss, and sickness. There are times when the spice of life loses its flavor. How do you react during such periods?

Once, for a family education course in archeology, I purchased kits containing replicas of ancient jugs, flasks, and bowls. Each artifact was deliberately broken, but the instructions said, "Anyone from 8 to 80" (Beware of this label!) could assemble the contents. The first family looked at the pieces of pottery and went home. The second family began, could not find a missing handle, and inconspicuously left the room. The third family struggled, expressed discouragement but, after several days, completed their project: a jug with visible cracks and empty spaces but a credible replica. What kind of person are you? When a segment of your life disintegrates do you walk away? Do you attempt to restructure but lose patience? Hope? Or, like the third family, do you gather up the fragments and rebuild.

For thirty years as a clergyman I have been a collector of broken dreams. Congregants, friends, strangers sit in my study and share their disappointments. But I also encounter those who go forth and begin again, recomposing the notes of their life into a symphony for the future.

Life never returns unto itself. That which is broken may not be made whole but there are always remnants, usually many in number, that can give pleasure and promise fulfillment. Make a list or a mental note of all that is good in your life. Shape and reshape the pieces. Life can take on many forms.

Anyone can be an artist of time.

Please Call if You Find the Missing Points

It's Okay to Be Imperfect

"**D**ID YOU EVER FIND THE TWO POINTS?"
    That's the wonderful feature of childhood friends. You might not see one another for ten years, but a few words, a sentence, and you feel you have never been apart. Like the question, "Did you ever find the two points?"

When, at the age of fifty-five, Alan asked me if I had ever found the two points. he was asking another question. "Did you finally forgive yourself?"

It was 1953 and I had transferred to the Albany Academy, a competitive college prep school where, even in the so-called apathetic fifties, we worried about grades, Ivy League colleges and our future. I handled the course load at the Academy. First year German: "Der, Die, Das; Des, Der, Des; Dem, Der, Dem; Den, Die, Das." American History: "Name ten major events in the Hoover Administration." Literature: "Before reading *Moby Dick* you might be interested in knowing that Herman Melville attended the Academy." I was not interested before or after reading *Moby Dick,* but, in later years I bragged, "The Albany Academy, best years of my life. Went there with Herman Melville." The English Department at Brown University scoffed at my fish story but. . . .

Only geometry proved difficult. At an early age I had decided on the rabbinate and abandoned math, except for the numbers 900 (age of Methuselah), 7 (days of Creation and days in the week), and 40 (length of a well-known flood and Moses' trek up Mount Sinai). "Pi r^2," "radius," "isosceles," "hypotenuse" reeked of strange worlds. My lack of interest accounted for a first quarter grade of B+, a decided blemish on my college application. Chagrined, I reapplied myself to the mysteries of geometry, even forsaking the "Howdy Doody Show" on our neighbor's television.

Study paid off. On my midterm geometry exam I received a 98 and an "Excellent" scrawled above my name in red pencil. Pop Webber, the math teacher, patted me on the back and I felt that special glow of geometric achievement. I cavorted down New Scotland Avenue and pranced into my home. "Dad! Dad!"

My mother answered: "He'll be home in an hour, Daniel."

I waited on the curb until I saw my father approach in the brown Plymouth sedan (that lost its canvas top in a windstorm on State Street hill) and thrust my test into the car window. Dad looked at the paper. He looked at me. He turned the paper upside down. He stroked his chin. I waited for the accolades. "Good, Daniel, good. 98. More than respectable." I beamed until he asked, "Who got the other two points?"

How do you answer that question? "Who got the other two points?" My father did not get the one point. I had mastered geometry. If the rabbinate fell through I could be an astrophysicist, a math wizard, an accountant! Everyone would point at me as I walked the streets of Albany reciting logarithms.

"Who got the other two points?" Bah!

Of course I knew my father was proud of me. That was Dad's sense of humor. Dry, wry, and pointless. Two pointless. But the question touched a sensitive nerve and every once in a while (when I'm not reciting logarithms) the words float across my mind. "Who got the other two points? Why weren't you a perfect 100?" Over the years part of me has searched for the missing points, the score to validate expectations long ago transferred from father to son.

So, Alan, when you ask me, "Did I find the two points?" I answer, "No." Sorry, Alan, I have never quite reached the standard set for me, unconsciously, in those early days at the Albany Academy. Or before. And I never will. But finally I can forgive myself. It has taken many years but I can forgive myself. I can celebrate a 98 instead of berating myself for the missing points.

"You've come a long way, Dan."

"Right!" I even admit I'm imperfect. There! I've said it. "I'm imperfect!"

However, any information leading to the capture of the missing two points would be greatly appreciated.

Thank you.

Being human means admitting we are not perfect. Often we hide this fact from ourselves and others. We become defensive. After a long day at work we yell at a loved one then try to rationalize our actions with an excuse, instead of acknowledging that we are under stress—or human. "Sorry, I can't take that job assignment. Out of my field." "Sorry, son, I am technologically inept. I can't put your computer together." "Sorry, I lost it. I lost it. I lost it!" We cannot be good to others until we can be good to ourselves and this implies accepting our imperfections, attempting to change what we can change but forgiving ourselves our limitations.

Occasionally when I read the *New York Times*, I count typos. They lurk in every column of this premier newspaper. Then I count the typos in myself. I take a reality check. I permit myself a typo. Then, at the top of my voice (but not in a library!) I shout, "I am imperfect!" Usually a chorus responds.

The artisans who weave beautiful Persian rugs intentionally insert one black thread in the intricate pattern of colors. At first glance the thread may not be evident, but look closely. It is there. The thread reminds the artist that an imperfection resides in his masterpiece as it does in all of life. However the black thread does not diminish the beauty of the Persian carpet and it does not mar the beauty of life.

We all have one black thread. Maybe more. We are all missing two points. Forgive yourself. Move forward. Look beyond the imperfection and cherish your intrinsic worth.

PART 3

BE CAREFUL OF THE RUT YOU CHOOSE

Breaking Old Patterns

Be Careful of the Rut You Choose

Break Out!

A T 7:00 A.M., DECEMBER 1, the friendly beep of my son's pocket organizer nudged me out of bed. After dressing quickly I drove along Route 8 to meet Bruce at the shed of the Horicon Highway Department.

A man of few words, Bruce puffed on his pipe, threw me a parka, and motioned for me to follow him into the depth of the cavernous garage where piles of sand and snow plows foretold winter. Wind sweeping down from Canada penetrated the cracks of the tongue-in-groove building; a warm-up, or chill-down for what was to follow.

Bruce disappeared behind a mountain of sand then reappeared dragging a battered metal sign. "Give me a hand, Dan," and we tossed the sign into the back of his red Ford pick-up next to a Remington rifle, there in case we spied a deer. "Hop in." I pushed his volunteer fireman's gear to one side, accustomed myself to the smell of stale beer and held on as we lumbered up Pease Hill Road, stopping next to a dirt road.

Bruce and I sometimes shared country philosophy. Today he said, "Don't have any words for you but this sign I'm going to put up—well, it says a lot. Help me nail it to that pine tree. The one over there where the dirt road begins."

I held a sign rusting on one side and dented in the middle.

Bruce hammered nails into a tree already scarred with holes. "Been doing this job for fifteen years," Bruce mumbled as he pulled his Exxon cap tighter on his head. "Fifteen years. Always on the same day. December 1. That's about the time this dirt road begins to freeze for the winter. Now its all soggy from the rains; have to wear boots if you want to slosh through. But another week or two? The ruts from the logging trucks, they'll be frozen solid, hard as rock and they'll stay that way until the spring thaw when the ice goes off the lake and the geese come back. Get caught in one of those deeper ruts in winter, you might as well go home and come back in three or four months. That's why the town put up this sign."

Bruce hammered in the last nail as mud oozed around his Dunham boots. Then he stepped back and admired his work. His leathery face broke into a half smile. "If you ask me, the words on that piece of metal there, they tell a lot about the way I'd want to live life."

The weak winter sun reflected off the green metal sign but the words boldly warned all travelers.

"BE CAREFUL OF THE RUT YOU CHOOSE.
YOU MAY BE IN IT FOR A LONG TIME."

Bruce chuckled and pulled the hood of his parka over his cap as flakes of snow filtered down through the pines.

"Someday I might retire from the highway department. Start a business. Miniature signs, *'BE CAREFUL OF THE RUT YOU CHOOSE, YOU MAY BE IN IT FOR A LONG TIME.'* Might even get one of those 800 numbers. How's 1-800-WAR-NING?"

I laughed and assured Bruce there would be customers. Personally I know many people who, long ago, became frozen in their ways and could benefit from a reminder.

BE CAREFUL OF THE RUT YOU CHOOSE.
YOU MAY BE IN IT FOR A LONG TIME!

Are you a potential customer for Bruce's sign? To evaluate your status please fill out the following questionnaire.

Name

Date

Check the appropriate box:	YES	NO
Am I doing work I no longer wish to do?	☐	☐
Have I continued in a failed relationship?	☐	☐
Have I grown in the last year? *(If you answer "yes" list the ways)*	☐	☐
Have I fulfilled any inner pursuits in the past year?	☐	☐
Is time moving past me?	☐	☐
Do I continue to be agitated over past events?	☐	☐

If you answered "yes" to any of the above estimate the amount of time wasted on nonproductive habits. A periodic check may be sufficient warning.

Ruts sneak up on us and before we know what has happened we are stuck. Day follows day, year follows year and eventually patterns become hardened and deadly.

An aside: The current fashionable car is the four-wheel-drive vehicle, a Jeep Laredo, Chevy Blazer, Ford Explorer. Even suburban women who only drive on flat roads and will never encounter mud or snow purchase four-wheel drives and sit in gas stations feeding the voracious appetite of these monsters. To appreciate the advantage of the four-wheel drive, watch a TV ad for Jeep. Bouncing over a rocky terrain, taking corners in deep snow, spraying mud in every direction the Jeep conquers the wildest elements. After viewing one of these ads a companion scoffed, "Four-wheel drives. A great invention. They permit you to get stuck further away from home and get in deeper." Two-legged-drive humans also have a way of becoming stuck, spinning our wheels ever deeper and depriving ourselves of fulfillment.

Before imitating a Jeep, examine your unhealthy routines (patterns stifling growth) and set yourself the challenge of breaking free. For instance, if you are stagnating in a career, investigate new directions. The pragmatics of earning a living may necessitate continuing in your present position but there are ways to supplement your career, to gain expertise in areas that will expand possibilities, to augment nonwork-related endeavors. If a relationship falters approach the other person with a different attitude, discuss ineffective patterns. Some routine is a necessary and a comforting adjunct of life but when we cease growing we cease living.

Some years ago a popular movie, *Midnight Express*, focused on an American youth imprisoned in Turkey. Every day the prisoners were taken outside for exercise and told to walk in a clockwise direction. One day the young man, in a symbolic act of protest, walked counterclockwise, an action disturbing to the prisoners and the guards but liberating for the American. His routine was broken and although he remained a prisoner in body, he had gained freedom. Walking counterclockwise may be the first step in releasing yourself from habits that have dominated a lifetime.

Certain patterns remain outside our control, but many of the ruts that imprison us are the work of our hands—and we have the power to effect change. Self-imprisonment is vividly portrayed by the Eastern philosopher Gurdjieff. A man draws a circle around himself in the sand. Days pass and he believes he is a captive, unable to cross over the line. "Step over the line! It's easy! Step over the line!" But the man cannot. The line now circumscribes his spirit. Are the patterns that dominate your life irreversible or have you drawn imaginary circles around yourself?

Step over the boundary, and if you need a prod, please call Bruce. He will send an autographed copy of his sign: "Be Careful of the Rut You Choose." Satisfaction guaranteed.

Walking the Maze

Sometimes Paths May Not Be Straight

A BRIDE IN AN IVORY COLORED SILK wedding dress with hand-sewn seed pearls descended the steps of Notre Dame de Chartres. As she paused for photographs, she gazed upward and traced the towering spires into the heavens, then rushed into a waiting horse and carriage.

When the wedding party had scattered I climbed the stairs of the cathedral at Chartres, a magnificent Gothic church that towers over its medieval village, stone bridges and tanneries. I had come to Chartres searching for a thirteenth century labyrinth designed in the floor of the nave. It was said that the maze of concentric circles, if stretched from end to end, would measure 851 feet. After wandering for some moments, unable to locate the design, I approached an art student sketching the kings of Judah on one small panel of the over thirty-thousand feet of stained glass windows that fill Chartres.

"Excuse me. Do you know where I may find the labyrinth?"

Putting his colors aside he led me to a square covered by rows of straight backed wooden chairs. "Here. The labyrinth is here, under these chairs."

In medieval times pilgrims to Chartres followed the route of this labyrinth on their knees. The torturous path of curves, torques, and switchbacks covered one-third of a mile, took at least an hour, and ended in the center at a rosette representing

Jerusalem. Once completed, the pilgrims achieved inner peace, a sense of calm. It was, one journeyer said, "A dance I do with my soul."

The age of pilgrimage at Chartres ended decades earlier and today only the eye can follow the maze, a journey broken by spindly wooden chair legs covering the floor.

The student rubbed hands streaked with charcoal on his jeans and looked at me quizzically. "You don't look like the kind of person who would go down on your knees."

I smiled.

"As long as I've been sketching here," he continued, "chairs have covered the labyrinth. Today visitors tour Chartres and listen to their guide: 'The nave reaches a record height of 121 feet.' They want to be comfortable, sit in chairs. Most of them never look beneath their feet." The young man's French accented English echoed in the stone cathedral. "To travel the maze on their knees? Even to walk the maze. No, monsieur, not today."

I studied the way to the rosette; the way to Jerusalem. The art student was correct. I am not the type to journey on my knees in a medieval church. But there are other forms of pilgrimage beside those to Chartres, Jerusalem, Lourdes, Compostella.

For instance, traveling into the intricate labyrinth of the self.

Few individuals wish to inquire: Who am I? What is the purpose of my existence? Where does my present road lead? Difficult, often disturbing questions.

If we summon the courage what will we find when we wend our way into the self? Jerusalem? Probably not. But we may find greater peace, less anxiety. An understanding of who we are and what we wish for our lives. Look into yourself.

On second thought, perhaps that *is* Jerusalem.

Few of us choose to embark on a maze. Instead of turns in the road we would choose straight paths, but sometimes they are marked with the sign "Dead End." We hear ourselves say, "This isn't working: my job, my marriage, my lifestyle," but we fear breaking away. What if we lose our way? What if we flounder in new relationships and uncertain careers?

When do you say, "It's enough—I will enter the maze of reevaluation"? Each person arrives at that point at a different stage in his or her life." Martin Luther went through a religious crisis before he called out, "Here I stand, I cannot do otherwise." We reach our own personal crisis and then we leave the familiar. If you have embarked on this journey you know that the first steps resemble an outing in a blinding snow storm or groping in the dark, but your newer voice commands, "Set out, set out." Hopefully you will listen.

In Greek mythology King Minos, the son of Zeus, had a wife who fell desperately in love with a handsome white bull. Their offspring, the Minotaur, possessed a human body and a bull's head. A labyrinth was built imprisoning the Minotaur on the Greek island of Crete. To pacify the beast a yearly tribute consisting of seven Athenian boys and girls was forced into the labyrinth. They would lose their way, only to be found and swallowed by the Minotaur. The finest of Athens' youth lost their lives until Prince Theseus entered the labyrinth and killed the Minotaur. Aware of the risk of becoming lost in the maze, Theseus uncurled a silken thread before entering. After killing the Minotaur he followed the thread back to daylight.

When you set off in new directions retain a tie with the known, a silken thread connecting you to the familiar—to a loved one, to a place where you feel comfortable, to a pattern of thought. The road to Jerusalem does not entail breaking away from all that is familiar. Who, or what, would permit you the confidence to set out? Establish a bond before leaving. Then unroll the silken thread of desperation tempered by hope and faith and seek new vistas.

What is the alternative? To find that tomorrow you will be where you are today. Is that what you desire?

Two thousand and nine hundred years ago God promised a nomadic patriarch named Abraham that he would become the father of a great nation if he obeyed God's instructions: "Get thee out of thy country, and from thy kindred, and from thy father's house." In other words, cut loose. In subsequent years Abraham traveled along a maze of desert trails and strange lands until he arrived at the Promised Land. Do you think Abraham wanted to forego the comfortable environs of his home in the Chaldean Mountains? But God had promised him a unique heritage if he set off on his long and sometimes circuitous journey. Why did he do it? To discover Jerusalem, the rosette at the end of his travels. It may have been safer to lead his flock through known pastures, but eventually the grass would disappear leaving only the deep ruts of a thousand footprints.

Plato taught, "We can easily forgive a child who is afraid of the dark; the real tragedy of life is when adults are afraid of the light." The light lies at the heart of the labyrinth.

Author in Residence

Open the Window of Life

RECENTLY I OCCUPIED THE COVETED CHAIR of "Author In Residence." The chair was a tiny wooden chair in the second grade classroom at St. George's School, Jerusalem. The teacher, Beth, had explained, "Dan, the children want to meet an author." Girded by erudite quotes on the art of writing I faced Samantha, a strawberry blond child from England; Gregory, a Fiji Islander whose smile was as round as his face; Said, a Palestinian from Jerusalem; and fifteen other seven and eight year olds. At first I was deeply flattered that all these children were sitting at my feet in order to glean wisdom, but I soon realized they always sat on the frayed Persian rug that covered the floor.

I shared the joys of being an author. Critical acclaim, recognition in such far away places as the Sinai desert, wealth. Not that I have experienced any of the above but I have heard from reliable sources. . . . Then I opened the floor (literally) to questions. Kevin, who had excused himself three times to go to the bathroom during my five minute talk, asked: "Mr. Author, how do you find enough to write about? The teacher said my story was too short."

"What was your story?" I asked the red-headed child who had more freckles than the walls of the Old City of Jerusalem had stones.

Kevin frowned. "About Fritz. He's the German shepherd next door."

"And?" I urged.

"He's mean. Very mean. Very, very mean. That's all I wrote. The teacher said she wanted more." Beth smiled.

"How many have Kevin's problem?" I asked.

Tiny hands shot up. I stood up, grateful to uncoil my body from the second grade school chair, and opened the window. Outside, the courtyard of the century-old building burst with the flowers of spring. The luscious aroma of the yellow broom plant rushed into the second grade room.

Turning back to the class I inquired, "What do you think will come into this window?" Yvonne, the daughter of a Nigerian diplomat, whispered: "A bee?" And, as if on cue (although not surprising in a city of miracles), a bee flew in the window, landing on the bulletin board where it remained until the class ended. "Any other thoughts?" Clark suggested dust would blow in from where they were repairing the street (accidentally uncovering Roman remains from the time of Jesus). To bees and dust we added sunflower seeds (Israel's "national nut"), a dove, an Israeli Airforce plane and the black alley cat dining in the green trash can.

After closing the window, I instructed Beth's class: "Now write a story about an open window." Charles spun the tale of an Israeli Airforce plane delivering sunflower seeds to St. George's second grade. Polly described a cat chasing a dove that chased a bee, then a German shepherd chased the cat that chased the dove that chased the bee. At days end we had created a class of authors in residence and, pleased with my success, I concluded the lesson: "Whenever you don't know what to write, open your mind, open your heart; they're windows to a wonderful world. Let ideas and feelings flow in. You will have plenty to write about."

I left the massive stone structure of St. George's School wondering whether Kevin, Samantha, Yvonne, and Charles had understood my final words about opening the mind and heart. Maybe they were too young. And how many of us, authors of our own mature lives, open mind and heart? Our lives can be dull. One sentence. "He's mean—very mean—very, very mean." One pattern of actions. Thoughts hardened over decades, feelings deadened. To avoid this dilemma, open windows. Most limits are of our own making.

But that's only the suggestion of Mr. Author, who, for one day, enjoyed the esteemed position of Author in Residence at St. George's School, Jerusalem, Israel.

I am the only person in Mount Kisco who owns an elephant.

Unlike most elephants, this elephant measures four by six inches and is made of wood. The stomach has a false bottom and when opened dozens of little elephants ranging in sizes from one-eighth to one-half-inch tumble out. From one elephant I have produced more pachyderms than could ever fit in a trunk (an elephant's trunk). Watching the elephants emerge I dream of snake charmers in a market in Old Delhi drawing a cobra out of a basket.

My wooden elephant reminds me of the human mind. (Except for the fact that the elephant never forgets.) Our mind teems with ideas of every size waiting to spill out and add spice to our days. All we need to do is open the latch on the door. How? By asking questions. "What can I do today that breaks the pattern of days past?" "What talents do I have that may supplement my life?" "Who can I be with today that will add stimulation, energy, and excitement?" The mind offers a release from routines that threaten to restrict our lives.

Every parent who has lived in the same house for many years can point to a wall covered with little pencil marks. A child stood against that wall and periodically his growth was measured. 3'7", 4'3", 5'. We measure physical growth but how often do we measure intellectual or emotional growth? If we do we may be disappointed.

William James wrote: "Many of us think we are thinking when we are only rearranging our prejudices." Not only our prejudices. Our ideas. Instead of opening ourselves to new thoughts, we twist, we turn, we reshuffle the amount of ideas we own, instead of permitting ideas to flow. That's also why our life stories may be too short; a repeat of stories played out over and over.

When I write I begin with a clear idea of how I want to proceed, but suddenly words pop out all over the place. I'm in free flight with hundreds of little elephants disguised as words (or vice versa) hopping around on my yellow pad. Once I open that window I am reborn—and never bored. The writing may or not work but I am headed off on new adventures, freed from the predictable. Find your own creative talent, painting, tennis, analyzing the world of numbers and uncover the rich vein of life.

A disciple of Michelangelo once asked the great artist how he could take a rough unhewn block of stone and create the statue of Moses in Rome, of David in the Academy at Florence. Michelangelo replied, "I see a work of art in every block of stone. It is there, waiting to be uncovered. My challenge as an artist is to chip away the covering and reveal the grandeur, the beauty." There is a grandeur in each one of us. Discard the empty rituals, the recurrent veneer, the constant refrain, "I have a dog. He's very mean."

Life has the potential to be a constant awakening in the ways we think and the ways we act. Henry David Thoreau tells the story of a beautiful insect that emerged from the dry leaf of an old apple-wood table. The table had stood in the farmer's kitchen for sixty years, but as appeared by counting the layers of wood, its origins could be traced to a far earlier time. Perhaps the heat of an urn hatched an egg hidden in the table. Whatever the explanation, an insect gnawed its way out after a hibernation of many decades. "Who knows what beautiful and winged life, whose egg has been buried for ages . . . may unexpectedly come forth? Only that day dawns to which we are awake. There is more day to dawn."

If you awaken who knows what you, or I, will find? Open the windows of the mind. Open the windows of life.

Gridlock Alert

Methods for Moving Ahead

THE LAST TIME MACADAM'S LAW CAUGHT ME in its sticky clutches was near my temple an hour before 11:00 A.M. services. When I left Interstate 684, a half-mile from my destination, I experienced a lengthy back up. A policewoman in a bright orange vest guided drivers through the morass, waving a flag to the right, to the left, gracefully, like the 6:00 A.M. aerobics class on Channel 7. In spite of her valiant efforts the traffic stalled. So near and yet so far.

Jim, who accompanied me from Armonk, calmly suggested we evaluate the situation. He could afford to be calm. He would not be called upon to deliver a sermon. I also suspected he relished the possibility of missing services. "Forgive me, O Lord, for my suspicions."

"Dan," he consoled, "As a man constantly called upon to consider options" (he traded on the options market), "here are the alternatives.

"We can follow the detour signs. A right at Kenilworth, a left on North, two more lefts and we're at the temple. I was caught in this yesterday."

I sighed. "Remember, there's the golf classic this weekend, somewhere near your second left!"

"True," Jim agreed, salivating at the thought of playing golf, driving a ball into the sky instead of sending prayers into heaven. "True. Well, let's reconsider."

He paused. "What if we walk? I know that's slow but we'll get there. Maybe another congregant will pick us up; although I suppose the whole congregation's tied up in this bottleneck." A slight exaggeration, since the whole congregation was probably playing golf.

Suddenly Jim's face brightened. "Why not hold today's services tomorrow?" This made some sense, but for the last three thousand years Sabbath services were held on the Sabbath.

Frustrated with my refusal to follow his sage wisdom Jim exclaimed: "Well, let's just wait here. Eventually this gridlock's bound to break." We did. And it did.

Since that day Jim teases me whenever we meet. "What is it Dan? Detour? Walk? Postpone today until tomorrow? Wait?" Of course he was only talking about the gridlock on Westchester Avenue. But what about gridlocks in life? Those times when we can't move forward. What then?

Everyone experiences gridlock. For instance:

1. A conversation between parent and child.
    "Be home at 12:00."
    "Why? I'm a senior in high school."
    How is this situation resolved?
2. "You only love work. When did you spend time with the family?"
    "But dear, how can we pay the mortgage, finance the BMW, save for the children's college?"
3. "I want to live in the city."
    "I want to live in the country."
4. "I've finished my part of the project; the others— they're holding me up."
5. "How can I be two places at once?"
6. "Sam, why do we always have the same argument?"

This list is only a starter.
Gridlock occurs when we seem unable to find resolution;

when we are stuck at a certain point in the dialogue with ourselves or others.

While sitting in my car near Interstate 684 and watching the gridlock expand in every direction I perceived that it is easier to create than to break a gridlock. I also observed different responses to gridlock.

The Honker. The honker leans on his horn, beats on his horn, presses his horn, with one long blow, a series of short staccato thrusts. The honker rests for thirty seconds and lulls the neighboring cars into a false sense of quiet. Then he coaxes the mother of all blasts from the horn, followed by cursing, yelling, beating on the dashboard. Does anything happen?

Final score: Gridlock, 33. Honker, high blood pressure.

My mother never learned to drive but she qualified for honker status when she encountered one of those glass ketchup bottles with the narrow opening that refused to release the ketchup. Well into her old age my mother would attack the ketchup bottle, banging on the side, the bottom, the table. Eventually she turned redder than the ketchup but nary a drop appeared. Ketchup gridlock. What to do?

On a more serious note I received a letter from an irate mother whose son had, the previous year, been rejected at my Alma Mater. The mother complained that her son was better qualified than the matriculating freshmen, a questionable conclusion. The mother's inability to let go, not of her son but of her anger, affected her own life and the happiness of the son who attended a fine midwestern university.

The honker leads a life of frustration characterized by noise, anger, regrets and a situation that will not change.

The Detourist. This type of person discovers alternate ways to circumvent the traffic jam. Once again I will illustrate with the ketchup bottle. Mother, in the wee hours of the night, created ingenious solutions to the annoying bottle. Detours. "Daniel, I have it! I'll write Heinz and tell them to put a zipper on the side of the bottle," or, "Why don't they make the opening wider?" I encouraged my mother to write Heinz. They would be forever indebted to her. She did not. I even spoke with my friend Bob, an accomplished teacher who, in his spare time, perfected the secret of coaxing ketchup out of a bottle. According to Bob, if you tilt the bottle and lightly tap the neck the ketchup flows in an even stream. My mother would have nothing to do with Bob's expertise. She was a honker, not a detourist. One of my great regrets in life is that Mother died before the invention of the plastic squeezable ketchup bottles.

If you wish to restore flow in your life, don't holler and bang. Find a more productive approach. If there is insufficient time to complete a project, rather than fuming within, work out a compromise, ask for an extension. If a child does not respond to your anger perhaps there is another way to communicate. Instead of yelling at your workaholic spouse, entice him or her back into the family by increasing the joy of being with family. Be a detourist.

The Walker. The walker leaves his car by the side of the road and sets out by foot. Although this may not work on a superhighway, or on the West Side Highway in New York where your car may be stripped before you return, the process is valid. The honker desires immediate results. The walker scales down expectations; does less, works slower, defers the goal, and refuses to be stymied by the vagaries of time.

In slowing down his world the walker recognizes the importance of timing. If angry with someone assess the proper moment to voice your concern. Step back from your immediate reaction and ask yourself, "Why am I angry, confused, at a standstill?" Sleep on your decisions. Next to my bed I keep pen and paper. Usually, at 3:00 A.M., inspiration travels around Mount Kisco and finds a crack in my 150-year-old farm house. Poof! The answer to the unsolvable. Caught on a sheet of paper. Don't force the issue. You will get there! Slowly.

The Yielder. That's right, sometimes you have to yield to gridlock. Certain problems refuse to vanish. Like Thanksgiving traffic on the Throgs Neck Bridge into New York. The yielder summons the courage to say to himself, "I'll live with it."

I have a friend who never travels without maps, guidebooks, and detailed reservations. Determined to avoid gridlock he is prepared for any eventuality. Ironically, he always finds himself in some situation where he feels helpless. Air New Guinea lands in Bora Bora instead of New Guinea. Le Gourmet Restaurant closes because the diners suffered a mysterious stomach ailment. The first rain storm in forty years soaks the Sahara when he's perched on a camel. Stymied. Gridlocked.

Life has occasions when we cannot move, when we have to wait it out, but eventually the gridlock will ease because life overflows with surprises and everything changes. In the meantime be a yielder, accept the fact that certain situations lack resolutions.

That's it. Four ways to respond to gridlock. The Honker goes nowhere. The Detourist finds another route. The Walker arrives slowly. The Yielder waits. Which one are you? Please communicate your answer. I can be found wherever road work occurs in the New York area.

Sunflowers

Turn Until You Find Brightness

IT WAS LATE SUMMER WHEN I FOLLOWED a path in southern France, near the town of San Remy. The way twisted in and out of olive orchards and vineyards. A sultry smell of lavender and thyme drifted over the fields and in the distance stone farmhouses led up to a village. I imagined a medieval chateau looking down on a square, old men smoking Gitane cigarettes and lounging under the broad branches of a plane tree.

My view was blocked as I disappeared into a grove of black cypress trees, just before the path led me to the place where a magnificent golden landscape emerged. A field of sunflowers stretched to the distant horizon. Sunflowers follow the sun and, since it was early morning, they faced in my direction where the path skirted the eastern side of the field. Row after row of blossoms awakening from nighttime stretched toward the sun. One hundred years ago Vincent Van Gogh painted this scene, casting paint on canvas as he flirted with madness.

When the sun reached its midday zenith I rested in a clearing among the flowers, then in late afternoon returned to my chateau on the western side of the field. Again the sunflowers seemed to follow me as they bowed to the slowly descending sun. As nighttime fell the blossoms bent toward the ground, at peace with their days journey and anticipating a new awakening.

During my stay in Provence I often wandered in fields of

sunflowers, charting their unending progress from east to west. Gradually I cultivated the harmless conceit that the sunflowers waved to me as I spent mornings on eastern trails; bowed to me as I spent afternoons on western trails. I experienced a joy in becoming one with a golden panorama.

Now, far from Provence, with only a single sunflower in a pot on my porch to remind me of those days, I miss the sunflowers' dance of life; but the philosophy of the field of sunflowers brightens my years; a philosophy communicated not by words but by actions. Follow the sun. Instead of standing in shadows, feeling life is hopeless, seek the sun. Instead of submitting to a life of boredom and apathy, let the full expanse of your own blossoms emerge into the light. None of us has opened as fully as we might. None of us ever will. Rather than relinquishing the power to grow, to take life into our own hands, discover the light and move in that direction. The sun is always there if only we turn.

And, if you wish a model to follow, spend a day in a field of sunflowers. It may change your life forever.

We cannot always follow the sun. Nighttime interferes. The challenge is to prevent night from sneaking up on us before we have adequately exhausted daylight. Albert Schweitzer taught, "An optimist is a person who sees green lights everywhere while the pessimist sees only the red lights. A truly wise person is colorblind." Life consists of red lights and green lights, but time triumphs over us when we fail to go forward at the green light. The sunflower, blessed with the intuitive wisdom of nature, finds the sun until the sun no longer exists. Don't let time sneak up on you and plunge you into nighttime.

When sorrow intercedes in our life we hear the expression, "Time will heal." I remember a man who had experienced a tragic loss. "Everyone said the only cure is time," he scoffed. "Well, every week I look at the clocks in my house and I listen to the pendulum tick and the chime ring. Days pass. Weeks. What happens? My pain persists. Whatever the clock says, it is always nighttime."

There should have been hours of daylight but, for this

man, there was only nighttime. Why? I asked his family. "Dad won't do anything to help himself," they answered, "He expects healing to come. He will sit in his rocking chair puffing on his pipe and healing will come. That's what he thinks. So far it hasn't worked."

A nautical friend cautions, "If you are in danger of crashing against rocks in a rough sea, pray to God." Then, with a twinkle, my friend adds, "But row away from the rocks." You are a partner in life and if you wish to avoid being swept under by the unrelenting force of time, help yourself. Row away from the rocks.

With the aid of nature the sunflower intuits the direction of the sun, but humans face a greater challenge. We are like a Nikon I own. The camera focuses automatically but sometimes the lens zooms in and out, in and out, searching for the clarity of subject. Then the shutter releases. All of us experience periods when it is difficult to focus on the light, but instead of placing lens caps over our lives we can seek the brightness—eventually we will focus. Where does brightness lie in your life? Have you actively sought to focus on these areas? Family? Nature? Music? Or do you lament the nighttime?

While on sabbatical I invented an ingenious way to outwit time. Actually the key was given to me by a French woman, Francoise, when we sat on a mound of poppies in the Israeli countryside. The sparkling red flowers, white daisies and the fragrance of the yellow broom plant brought springtime to a landscape pockmarked with black basalt stones. These stones were all that remained of buildings dating to the year 700 B.C.E.

Our picnic site was a tel; the layers of a vanished civilization, and the stones came from the ancient town of Lachish, lying in ruins. Two thousand and seven hundred years ago Lachish stood as the last town in the way of Assyria's march on Jerusalem. Men with the crossword puzzle names of Sennacherib and Sargon with their armies marched against Lachish—but not to sit among fields of spring flowers. Since the destruction Lachish stands barren, except once a year when the flowers blossom. Man can build cities; man cannot imitate nature's display.

There is sadness to springtime in Israel. Soon the burning

Mediterranean sun advances over the countryside. The petals of the poppy float aimlessly in the breeze and the tall thistle encroaches. The scorched fields brown out for another year. I mentioned this to Francoise, intently photographing a poppy half awakened from its bud. She nodded and asked,

"Where do you go after leaving Israel?"

"Provence. In two weeks."

"Perfect!" she exclaimed. "When you arrive in France springtime will again greet you. Do not be sad."

Francoise knew the seasons and on a day in France when the sky, painted a deep blue, embraced the French countryside, I delighted in my second spring in one year. The green Citroën followed quiet roads and the deep smell of the broom wafted through open windows. I wandered in lush fields, among ancient city remnants; this time Roman not Israelite. Fields of poppies stretched from Avignon to Aix en Provence and I wondered, "Do the flowers of Israel really die or do they steal away and come to France?" On my final day in France a field of sunflowers opened their golden blossoms and basked in the sunlight.

Could life be more magnificent than pursuing spring? From Israel to France to wherever the winds of time travel in their unceasing journey. Only a sabbatical permitted me the whimsical six-month springtime. I knew that eventually I would be overtaken with dying thistles. But, for one year I had tricked time. At the very moment time wanted to turn the landscape brown I had made my escape! Found spring. Found the sun. And now, writing these words on a cold, overcast November day I still have the confidence that I can introduce springtime into my life whenever I ask, "Does life have to be filled with darkness?" Usually I answer, "No", and within my heart I pursue a springtime bursting into red poppies and yellow sunflowers.

Are you despondent? Sad? Do you imbue your life with an overriding futility? Does it need to be that way? Have you turned and turned until you found the sun? What can bring cheer to your life?

Learn from the sunflower.

A Tennis Spin

Look at Life with New Eyes

ONE REASON MANY OF US LIVE IN the dark is our refusal to see the light. This was a truth I learned many years ago while a student at a seminary in Cincinnati, Ohio. The teacher was my professor of Old Testament, Dr. C., affectionately called "Distinguished Professor of Genesis, Exodus, and Tennis." Professor C. loved Bible. He also loved tennis and at the time when I was a student, Dr. C. was frustrated in his sport. Why? Because every day he walked past an immaculately groomed tennis court with a sign swinging from the gate

MEMBERS ONLY

NO

VISITORS PERMITTED

Professor C. was a devout man who followed his own teachings, especially the Ten Commandments. With one exception. The Tenth Commandment. The one about not coveting your neighbors wife or ass or anything that belongs to your neighbor. He was okay when it came to wives and asses but he did covet the pristine red clay of his neighbor's tennis court and, whenever he passed by, words of lamentation escaped his mouth. "Woe, unto me," which translated into: "Why does the sign read

MEMBERS ONLY

No

VISITORS PERMITTED"

But it did and Dr. C. contented himself with bouncing a bright yellow Wilson tennis ball off the pavement in front of the court.

Until that day when a third-year student, Elijah Nance from Nevada, burst into chapel and called out, "Dr. C.'s playing tennis on the court with the sign

MEMBERS ONLY

No

VISITORS PERMITTED"

With a chorus of "Amen," we stormed onto Clifton Avenue, racing toward the tennis court. When we arrived Dr. C., wearing white shorts, a white T-shirt and, a white skull cap that kept the sun out of his eyes had just lobbed a ball over the fence into the back seat of a Plymouth Convertible stopped at a traffic light at the corner of Clifton and Ludlow.

While Elijah went to retrieve the errant ball we asked Dr. C., "Sir, how can you play on this court? Have the rules changed? Did you receive special permission?" Our revered sage pulled his socks higher on his spindly legs and motioned for us to gather around. "Dear students," he began, swinging his wooden racket, "As you are well aware, for many years I have longed to play on this court and for many years the sign prevented me from entering the Promised Land. Last night I had a revelation. God's work here on earth is never finished."

We sat, puzzled at this cryptic remark.

"The signmaker who wrote

MEMBERS ONLY

NO

VISITORS PERMITTED

also did not finish his work. He left out the punctuation. For years I have read,

MEMBERS ONLY

NO

VISITORS PERMITTED

but what about the missing punctuation marks? Why did the signmaker leave out punctuation marks. Because he wanted *me* to insert the marks. With this revelation commas, periods, question marks shot into my vision like balls shooting out of a ball machine. Punctuation fell into place at the end of each phrase. From that point on I read the sign in a new way:

MEMBERS ONLY?

NO!

VISITORS PERMITTED."

Hitting a vicious backhand into the net, Dr. C. concluded. "That's why I am playing tennis on this court. Always remember, my disciples, there is more than one way to read a sign."

I don't recollect much of Dr. C.'s learned discourse on Genesis and Exodus but I will never forget the spin he put on life. Often we stand in the dark because we refuse to look in a different direction, refuse to read signs from another perspective. Look at your life from another angle. It may be a whole new game.

Marcel Proust cautions, "The voyage of discovery lies not in seeing new landscapes but in having new eyes." Doctor C., after years of perceiving the sign in the same tired way, suddenly acquired new eyes. Often a small change in perspective, a comma, a period, a question mark can turn our world around. A long hike consists of small steps. The transformation of old patterns begins with barely perceptible revisions. We may walk by a painting we have seen many times but when we look from a different angle we notice a new color and shape. A friend, a stranger shares a word and we gain sudden insight. Instead of simply hearing a loved one we listen and for the first time gain an understanding of their needs. Consider these questions: "Is there another way to approach a friend, or someone with whom you feel uncomfortable? Is there another approach to a problem?" The answers might enhance your life. Some people travel all over the world, from Cape Cod to India, but wherever they go the world is viewed from their own provincial perspective. Others never leave their community but their landscape is diverse and exciting because they see that world with constantly renewed eyes.

During a recent eclipse a friend and amateur astrologist, Albert, called his wife Nina. "I made plans for our October vacation. You'll adore it. Tell you when I see you at 6:00." Nina imagined the golden beaches of Hawaii, an intimate cafe in Montmartre, the hills of Tuscany and, at 6:00, waited for her husband in the lobby of their East 71st Street townhouse.

"Well!" she exploded when Albert rushed through the front door, waving airline tickets. Nina studied the coupons stapled together by the travel agent, looked up at Albert, looked back at the coupons. "India?" she gasped, "India? Romantic? That's the only country in the world I never wanted to visit. Poverty. Dysentery. Heat."

"Now, now, Nina," Albert soothed. "That's an exaggeration. I know you'll love it!" With that "we" decision Albert and Nina flew Air India to New Delhi—but not for the classic tour of the land of the Raj. Albert, an accountant with a passion for astronomy, wanted to witness a total eclipse of the sun. He had convinced Nina after explaining, "A total eclipse from any one place in the earth occurs once in three hundred and sixty years I don't expect to be here in 2355. Anyway, think how impressed your friends will be. This, my dear wife, is unique!"

When Albert returned he described the eclipse. "Here we were, Nina and I, fifty miles from the Taj Mahal in a mudbrick village with Indians in colorful saris, a Sikh, his uncut hair knotted in a bun under a turban, a stockbroker from New York and astronomers from California. Two minutes before the eclipse a middle aged Indian from New Delhi, bundled up in a blanket, began the countdown. 'Two minutes. One minute. Thirty seconds.' The moon had already passed across most of the sun, and only a sliver of light protruded. Shadows had descended over the desert landscape. Everyone wore special sunglasses or looked through film to protect their eyes. "Twenty-five seconds. Twenty, fifteen, ten, five." Exactly on schedule the sun disappeared and day became night. Some people clapped, others gasped. For almost a minute we were one, all of us standing close together. Gradually the sunlight returned. What a sight! I think even Nina was impressed. At any rate she promised to return with me in three hundred and sixty years!"

Curious, I asked Albert. "How do the Indians explain an eclipse?"

Albert considered my question. "The educated react like their colleagues all over the world but some of the villagers saw the eclipse as evil. Darkness over light."

Albert paused. "One Indian suggested that we should wear special glasses to protect ourselves from all the evil. Can't look at it directly. Interesting?"

I considered. I don't know much about eclipses but that Indian's theory applied to other aspects of life. We all encounter eclipses in our life. Not of the sun; of brightness and joy. Consider death, sickness, loss of a job, family stress. On those occasions our world turns black. How do we go on? With a new insight. Viewing our world through different glasses. Perhaps not directly. Perhaps through the reflecting lens of another person to offer advice and support. By wearing different glasses the world takes on a new shape; perhaps one better suited to where you are at a particular time. The stoic philosopher Epictetus taught, "I am upset not by events but rather by the way I view them."

One person will look out a window after a rainfall and see the drops of water still finding their way down the glass and onto the window sill. A second person will look beyond the window pane and see the sun shimmering off a pool of water or a rainbow. We cannot always control what happens to us but we can control the perspective. The next time you find yourself depressed ask, "Is there another way to look at what is happening to me? Is their another way to address my difficulties? Is there more than one way to interpret words?" If there is, then you might discover not only new eyes but a new and more welcoming future landscape.

Close your eyes. Open them. Enjoy the landscape.

Walking

Take One Step

EVERYTHING I EVER NEEDED TO LEARN about walking I learned from Bob. Over the years Bob has crisscrossed his home state of Connecticut, following a stone wall to a deserted well, picking his way on rocks across an icy stream, hiking on a logging road to a ghost town and often wandering aimlessly for the sheer love of walking. Bob taught me how to choose a sapling for a walking stick, whittling the wooden handle into a comfortable feel. My Gore-Tex boots, backpack and poly pro shirts bear Bob's imprint and he even explained why, without proper conditioning, Bad Muscles Happen to Good Walkers!

On a fall day, when a blanket of autumn leaves tucked the ground in for winter, Bob approached walking from a theological perspective. The occasion for Bob's remarks arose when I tripped over a fallen limb buried beneath a pile of leaves. "Watch yourself," Bob cautioned, "You can never take walking for granted," and with that comment Bob set forth on his theory: Walking and the Act of Faith.

"After all these years you never think about walking. Am I right?" I nodded. "When you walk along the road you relax. The last thought on your mind is putting one foot before the other."

We sprawled on a log cushioned by moss. "Then," Bob continued "you trip and for a second you are aware of your feet." A chipmunk scurried over the log, surprised to see visitors at his normal haunt. Bob continued, "Think of a child learning to walk. First he tests the ground and, unsure of what he will find, loses his balance and falls. Or an adult walking for the first time after breaking a leg; they're reentering the world of the walker. It takes a while to gain or regain trust. Correct?"

I agreed.

"Let's try an experiment," Bob suggested. "Stand up."

I rose. The back of my corduroys felt clammy from the damp moss.

"Take a step and follow your leg from the moment you raise your foot—that's it. Slowly. Slowly. Concentrate on your actions."

I felt myself falling, momentarily off balance, too conscious of my movements.

Bob smiled. The chipmunk had returned to the far end of the log, bringing some of its family, and Bob warmed to his subject.

"You see, walking, it's really not that easy. There is a split second when you lose control—you're suspended out there, hoping the ground will meet your step. Usually the ground responds, or rather your foot finds the ground. You never think about the act of walking, unless you are very young or very old, the most tenuous times on the cycle of life."

I nodded. "Isn't that faith, Dan? The certainty that each step will discover a firm footing. Faith?"

Bob added. "Every step we take in life calls for faith. Otherwise we would never take risks, move forward—afraid we might fall. Every life also has breaks, not in legs but in the worn patterns. We force ourselves to go out once more, in search of firm ground where we can place our feet. Can you imagine what would happen if we lived with the constant fear of falling? Life would stop."

We had gone over the heads of the chipmunks who scampered into brush, engaging in a game of hide and seek. And, since life consists of walking, not talking about walking, Bob and I took our walking sticks and went on down the path.

What is faith? The confidence that when you step out on nothing you will land on something. What is faith? The catalyst for breaking patterns and pulling yourself out of ruts. Why are we afraid to break longtime patterns that no longer work? Because we are afraid of what lies out there. Faith encourages us to take the step to break out of our tired habits.

One of the inspirations for my amateur career as an archeologist was Indiana Jones. In one movie, Indy is on the verge of redeeming the Holy Chalice but first he must cross a bottomless chasm. Indiana takes a step and, instead of falling into nothingness, a bridge mysteriously appears. Our hero crosses in safety. We fear leaving ruts because we do not know what waits out there, but usually a bridge appears. Where will it lead? Until we step out we will never know. Søren Kierkegaard stressed the need for a leap of faith. A single step will do.

When I was seven years old I took part in my first obstacle race at camp. I jumped over hurdles, climbed a tree (a little tree!), and swam to the raft. The final obstacle: I had to crawl under a tarp spread out on the ball field. To compound the difficulty a counselor directed water from a fire hose in front of each child, driving the tarp hard against the ground. (Today this activity would rank high on the list of summer camp child abuse!) I was afraid of the dark and the force of the water and questioned whether I would ever emerge. A counselor called out, "Go for it, Dan. Your father's a rabbi. Didn't he teach you faith?" At the age of seven how could I know faith is not genetic? Slowly I descended, stuck my head under the tarp, began crawling and exited on the other side. If we have faith we will come out safely on the other side. But first you have to take a step instead of standing by the edge.

That step never comes with guarantees. What have you accomplished of worth that comes with guarantees? The first step brings risks, in work, in love, in personal growth—but eventually we become accustomed to walking into freedom.

Bungee Jumping

Life Changes Even if You Do Not

K ENT WOOD AND I SAT IN THE COURTYARD of the Albright
Institute in Jerusalem and talked about my sabbatical.
"When you were in New Zealand," he asked, "did you
try bungee jumping?" A rather strange question from a Bible
scholar, but he explained that the year before he had lectured in
Christ Church and one of his younger colleagues invited him to
bungee jump.

"Did you?" I asked.

Kent laughed. "As the son of an Evangelical minister I
believe in God, but I don't believe in a bungee cord! Anyway, I'm
too old—and too afraid."

"Agreed," I nodded, "But at any age there must be fear.
Especially on that first jump. In New Zealand I spoke with a
young Canadian, on a bridge over the Dart River. The Canadian
was on his third jump. I asked him why he jumped and his answer
sounded like something out of *Zen and the Art of Bungee Jumping.*"

"There's something mystical about bungee jumping," my
young friend said. "Watch the way each person jumps."

"I looked up at the bridge where a suntanned employee of
Dart River Bungee Jumping fastened a cord around the feet of a
jumper. Confidently, the jumper spread his arms, soared like an
eagle into space and bounced up and down three or four times.

Finally, as he hung feet first over the river, a boat pulled him in. The second customer (I am inclined to say victim) jumped, her blue dress swept up by the downdraft. The third jumper, reluctant, was gently pushed off the platform. Video cameras ran furiously; only twenty seconds to record the jump for some distant generation to watch while a little towhead would exclaim: 'Grandpa you really did that!'

Then my Canadian guide to the thrills of bungee jumping, inserted his philosophical caveat: "I mean, the reason this is mystical is that everyone chooses their own way to jump but after a few bounces everyone ends up just where they began. Neat! I'd like to spend my life taking chances, jumping off, yet always tied to one place. Back where I began. The security. Understand?"

I looked at Kent who had picked up a copy of the *Oxford Bible*. "It says here that in the beginning God created the heaven and the earth. I can't find it written anywhere that afterward everything remained the same. Take it from me, your Canadian friend will revise his theory."

Kent smiled. "I've had my share of bounces in life. Ups and downs. Sometimes I've chosen to jump. To try something different. Other times I've been pushed. Events just shoved me off the platform. And I can tell you, you never end up where you began. Geographically? Maybe. But each one of life's experiences leaves a lasting effect. Often a scar. It's one thing to fall off a bridge in New Zealand, another thing to come back from the inevitable falls of life. No boat pulls you in. If you're going to right yourself you're going to do it on your own.

"Life changes, Dan. It's never what it once was. I'm not certain if that's good or bad but you can't deceive yourself. At least I can't. Your young friend might succeed for a year or two, maybe more, but one of these days he will discover that there's no cord holding him fast—that he's out there, just out there. But I don't know why I'm telling you all this. You're the preacher. I'm a professor of Bible."

At the risk of over-analyzing bungee jumping I would agree with Kent. We never end where we begin. Those who choose to remain in ruts and place their lives on hold find that life slips from under them. Try standing in the ocean. Dig your toes into the sandy bottom as waves wash onto shore and recede. The sand will shift under you. Eventually you will find yourself pulled out to sea. Only the illusion of nonmovement exists. Or try treading water for an extended period. It is easier to swim. In attempting to retain old patterns, hoping this will stop our world, we lose ground. As the first century philosopher Heraclitus taught, life is in constant flux. Whether or not we change we are changed by events around us. You may stop the hands on every clock in your house but you will not stop time.

One of the teachers in my religious school also teaches drivers ed in the local high school. I theorize that he teaches religion because he hopes prayer will save him from some of his drivers ed students. Once I asked Neil, "What scares you the most when you are sitting in a car with a novice driver?" He answered, "When they step on the brake."

"The brake?"

Neil explained. "I'm exaggerating but I find the worst accidents can occur when a student is too hesitant. He arrives at a crowded intersection, jams his foot on the brakes and cars slam into him from every direction. The experienced driver does not assume that when he stops everyone else will stop."

Neil laughed, "I'm also afraid when a student steps on the gas, backs up, goes forward, closes the door."

I understood Neil's answer, "When they step on the brake." He meant, flow with the traffic, flow with life.

According to a news story in the *New York Times*, in the 1996 election, in the town of Tunbridge, Vermont, retired farmer Fred Tuttle received two votes for President, five votes for U.S. Representative, six for Governor, one for Lieutenant Governor and fourteen for high bailiff. Who is Fred Tuttle? A 77-year-old dairy farmer who was a write-in candidate supported by Vermonters who saw him in a locally made movie about a retired farmer running for Congress. Mr. Tuttle has enjoyed his stint as a celebrity. Before the movie his only topic of conversation was army service in Europe in World War II. Now his life is filled with adventure. When the movie opened in New York, Mr. Tuttle went to the city, ate tofu at a Chinese restaurant, was caught in the New York Marathon, and slept on a futon. He also manned a "Fred" booth at the Tunbridge World's Fair. For a brief moment Mr. Tuttle's life came alive.

The movie starring Mr. Tuttle (with friends Kermit Gliven, Euclid and Priscilla Farnham, and cats Snowball and Fluff) poignantly documented a vanishing Vermont. The family farm has disappeared, bought by New York millionaires; the quaint country store sells *Barrons Weekly* and rents VCRs to "the city folk" and Wal-Mart invades the countryside, staking out its claim next to Henry's Apple Stand. With the exception of Fred Tuttle, the old-timers rock on the porch of the general store and lament (justifiably?) the world slipping away from them. Back and forth. Back and forth. An immovable pattern.

An advertisement for an outboard motor included a disclaimer. "The outboard motor you have purchased has a slight mechanical problem. Sometimes, when you shift the lever in forward gear, you will have a strange sensation that you are in reverse. You are. We hope to correct this problem in the near future in order to assure that when you expect to move ahead you are not moving backwards. Thank you for your patience."

When we remain in a rut and fail to move forward we also go in reverse. Keeping pace with the rapid change of the 1990s has drawbacks, but if we do not adapt to some degree we slip backwards. We cannot hold our own.

So close this book, leave your comfortable couch and drive to the local video store. Rent a movie on bungee jumping. Enjoy, but don't be fooled by the illusion that anyone ends where he began.

You cannot stop time.

Captive in Cabo

Follow the Moonlight

S EVERAL YEARS AGO I VISITED CABO SAN LUCAS, the Mexican peninsula jutting into the Atlantic Ocean on one side, the Pacific Ocean on the other. One evening I noticed a line of tripods, perched like herons' necks, cameras on top, focusing on the Pacific. Since I never miss a photo opportunity I retrieved my camera from the room and joined the photographers—wondering what they were photographing. I asked the photographer standing next to me, a serious cameraman with a Hasselblad draped around his neck and a Nikon on his shoulder, "Are the whales migrating? Are dolphins jumping? Is there a sighting of the Queen Elizabeth?"

In answer the man said, "The sun. Watch the sun." And there, in a ball of red, the sun hovered above the Pacific, preparing for a magnificent departure. I shot the sunset. Bright rays caressed the ocean waters, turning the Pacific gold, pink, a deep purple. The sun tucked itself beneath a wave, asleep for the night. Did that stop me? No. Click. Click. Click. I finished off a fourth roll of film although there was nothing to see. What was I hoping? That the sun might rise for a final curtain call? One last wink? Was I unwilling to part with the day? Wanting more. Always wanting more.

Eventually I looked up. The other photographers had vanished. Then I heard voices and the click of shutters behind me, on the far side of the peninsula. My companions had crossed to the Atlantic where a full moon rose in a sky dotted with twinkling stars. I joined the photographers, watching the moon assume its position, a diadem above the constellations. Photographing the night sky was more difficult than photographing the setting sun, but with patience and the proper exposure I captured the brightness of the night; a far better pursuit than chasing pictures of a sun no longer present.

In all of our lives there are moments, years, when we experience loss; not of the sun but of the sunlight. Death and sickness take those we love beyond the horizon. We wish they would return for one final appearance but they cannot—or will not. Hesitant to acknowledge the changing seasons, hopelessly in love with spring, we refuse to cross over to the other side.

Even in loss there is a brightness. The moon, the presence of our loved one, still shines through loss. Memories twinkle like stars; reminders of joys shared in years past. The light of memory glows when all else seems dark and eventually nighttime passes; for some sooner than for others. A new day dawns, a day embracing its own hidden promise.

Cross over. Nighttime beckons with a special light. Grasp that light, then wait, wait for daylight.

Why do we hesitate to leave the sun when it no longer provides light? One reason may be that we are uncertain what lies on the other side. How can you know the moon will be there? When confronted by darkness what do you do? Some people stumble blindly, others find a candle or a flashlight. If the sun has vanished then the first way to adjust to this darkness is to consider the options, but it is at precisely this point that many become too narrow in their vision. "What can I do?" "How can I move forth?" We only see the sun that has vanished.

In Judaism, approximately eleven months after a death, the tombstone is unveiled at a special ceremony. A psychological component accompanies this ritual. The unveiling implies a closure.

Our grief may remain but the ceremony says, "Get on with it! One period has ended, the next must begin." This transition does not occur instantly. If you walk outside on a star-filled night it may take several moments to adjust to the stars, to find the moon—but they are there. If you look up. Unfortunately we tend to stare in only one direction and perpetuate a pattern long since dead.

How many revolutions of the earth will you permit to pass you by before you act? In my home town of Albany, New York, I was raised with the legend of Rip Van Winkle who slept for twenty years after playing ninepins with Hendrick Hudson and his crew of the *Half Moon*. When Rip finally awoke his world had changed dramatically. A postscript to Washington Irving's tale explained: "The story of Rip Van Winkle may seem incredible to many, but nonetheless I give it my full belief, for I know the vicinity of old Dutch settlements to have been very subject to marvelous events and appearances."

Washington Irving defines the marvelous event to be Rip's long sleep, but in reality I know many people who have been asleep for twenty years. They don't snore, they occasionally stretch, they may even go about the motions of life, but only the motions. Rip Van Winkle thrives in areas far removed from the Hudson River; wherever people fixate on the departed sun.

Tonight, instead of counting sheep (which is a rut of its own kind!), count the days you refused to see lights shimmering in the nighttime sky. Because, as my photographer friend might say, "That's a better picture."

Outward Bound

Let Go of Old Patterns

DEAR DAN,

I just moved to Vermont. Instead of rushing for the 6:37 from Scarsdale to Grand Central I drive twenty miles an hour behind a logging truck headed toward Sunapee. Not easy for a Type A personality.

I wasn't sure I could make the transition from a Wall Street law practice to a small country office until I went on an Outward Bound Adult Program in Maine. The first day we had to swing from a rope on one side of a crevice to a rope dangling on the other side. We were tied to a guide line. No real danger. Still . . . the first time I was afraid to let go of the rope. I dangled in the air. Our guide encouraged me: "Try again. You have to let go. It's the only way to reach the other side."

I did. For a moment my arms flailed in space and I thought I would fall. Then I reached out, seized the second rope, and jumped to the far side. On the way home I realized I had released more than a rope. I had pushed off from the security of my center hall colonial in Westchester, from loyal clients, friends from childhood. I'm not sure what I'll find in Vermont but I'm excited and I'm ready.

At least I've broken old patterns and that's a start.

Sincerely,

Bernie

Do you have the courage to ask yourself the questions Bernie asked before moving to Vermont? (1) What would my life be like if I left the city where I have lived for so many years? (2) Could I begin with a new firm or perhaps a new career? (3) Could I make new friends? And if I could not?

I admire those rare individuals able to ask these questions and, more importantly, to act upon the answers. Winston Churchill wrote, "Men stumble over the truth from time to time but most pick themselves up and hurry off as if nothing happened." We know we should change our behavior, the truth stares us in the face. But? To be brutally honest with the self is never a pleasant proposition. Like Bernie, we may grab hold of the rope, advance to the edge, then quickly return to a safe position on this side of the crevice. Who wishes to be outward bound? But the alternative, short-term safety, may create future chasms of despair and unhappiness. Perhaps it is easier to jump when the gap between where we are and where we want to be remains narrow, before we realize we have irretrievably compromised our life.

A disclaimer. I am not a real estate agent and I do not live in Vermont. I also deny any relationship, familial or otherwise, with Vermont real estate agents. In brief, I am not encouraging you to move to Vermont. Not even to move geographically. Being outward bound may occur within the mind or the heart. The jump occurs when you fill out the application that begins, "Are you where you want to be?" A negative answer qualifies you for outward bound. Congratulations!

RK

Be Yourself

I WAS BORN AN RK. FIRST GENERATION RK. Closely related to an MK or possibly a PK. What is an RK? A rabbi's kid, as an MK is a minister's kid and a PK a president's kid. We share the burden of an uncommonly high set of expectations placed upon us by everyone else. Expectations that very few people would place upon themselves.

For instance, as an RK playing with the "Dogwood Street Gang" was frowned upon, in modern vernacular, not Rabbinically Correct. The Dogwood Street Gang, as everyone knew, climbed on garage roofs, marked houses with shaving cream on Halloween, and was a generally rowdy lot. RK beware. I avoided the gang until one day I found myself shooting squirrels with a BB gun in the yard behind our house. Who can resist the lure of a BB gun? And there I was a Dogwood Street Ganger at last! I missed the squirrel and also missed the sound of a car pulling into the driveway. Too late I fled, tripped over a log and found myself in Dr. Silverman's office, the victim of a sprained ankle. The doctor asked, "How did this happen, Daniel?" When I told him the truth (RKs never lie!) Dr. Silverman (a member of my father's congregation) shook his head. Where had I gone wrong? If it had been my friend Donnie, well, what could you expect? But the rabbi's kid? This was not the only time I felt caught between conflicting choices; on one hand the subtle pressures incumbent upon the RK, on the other hand the pressure of peer acceptance. Looking back, I often followed my friends but the mantle of guilt spawned by RKism weighed heavily.

Throughout the years my special status attracted cautious reactions. In my freshman year at college I rushed a fraternity, an action emphasizing acceptance along the narrow halls of manhood. The pledgemaster, hoping to put me at ease, commented, "So you come from Albany. I hear they have a great red light district there." The brothers interrupted: "Hey Jim, don't you know Dan's father's a Rabbi? Cut the language."

In retrospect I can't be certain when the RK inoculation took but I would estimate at an early age. By the time I was nine I had become the Suffering Servant for everyone else's ideals, encumbered with expectations no one else could, or wanted to, fulfill. Of course I had my moments of rebellion. On Saturdays my friends went to the Madison Avenue Theater where the eighth chapter in the serial "The Lone Ranger and Tonto" placed the masked hero on the edge of a cliff, pursued by bandits. Would his horse Silver successfully leap across the abyss and escape the pursuers? I would never know. Instead I sat restlessly on the edge of my seat at temple, while my father intoned prayers destined to bridge the abyss between heaven and earth. While waiting for the silent prayer, I found a marble in my pocket and released the missile onto the wooden floor of the one hundred and forty-five-year-old sanctuary. Congregants chuckled as the red aggie rolled slowly down hill. Click. Click. Click. The marble finally landed, an offering at my father's pulpit. Dad sighed with relief until I let go with a second marble. But usually I did not roll the marbles of my life. Usually they were rolled for me while I fulfilled the model of proper behavior, academic achievement, and modesty. After all, I was an RK.

Beyond birth, what was the major influence transforming me into an RK? Parents? In fairness, my parents made every effort to protect me from RK status and respect my individual needs even when those needs ran counter to their wishes. For instance, my father, a product of the immigrant experience, believed strongly in public education and I followed this route until high school. In my sophomore year I pleaded for the opportunity to join my friends at the Albany Academy, not only a private school but a military country day school. Dad relented but I wonder what thoughts coursed through his mind when I appeared in his study dressed to kill. With sword and in full military paraphernalia. Ironically, he was preparing a sermon on public education as a leveler for classes, races, religions. And there I was, sword dangling at the side, a black plumed hat sporting slightly moldy feathers and shoes recently recovered from too much spit in the spit shine. On that day I was not a symbol of my father's convictions, not an extension of who he was. At least not on the outside. But despite my father's attempts, forces converge and we become an amalgam of what others wish us to be. Especially if we are the children of public figures.

There was only one step beyond being an RK and I took that step when I was eighteen, my father fifty-seven and dying. We sat in his study as the season passed and the red leaves on the maple tree signaled a time of barrenness.

"Daniel," my father asked, "Do you know what you wish to do with your life?"

I answered honestly. "I want to be a rabbi. Your life is the life I wish to live."

In one sentence I had bestowed the most precious gift a son can give, the affirmation of a father's life, the culmination of his dreams, if not his expectations. But my father did not seize the gift.

"Son, why do you wish to be a rabbi?"

I replied, "Because I want to serve people."

My father smiled. "There are many ways to serve. You do not need to be a rabbi."

As a gaggle of geese on their southern pilgrimage circled outside I knew my father was releasing me. Setting me free to be who I chose. He did not want to direct my future. He hoped he had not directed my past. But I would always be an RK and now the circle had reached completion.

Years have passed. RK and Rabbi fused inextricably and I have gained great satisfaction from my profession. But occasionally I attempt to define the fragments of the self that are genuine and untarnished? What parts of who I am have been shaped in the mold of others; fashioned on the anvil of time? Too late to unscramble. And futile. But occasionally, only occasionally, I contemplate another scenario; a lifetime spent as an OK, an ordinary kid. A tabula rasa exempt from all expectations. As if that species ever exists.

If you were to define yourself, how many qualities would be unique to you and how many the result of external influences? What are you? Who are you? In the years allotted to you have you used time in a way proper for you, or proper for someone else? What percentage of your life was and is your life? Time slips by and, when we look back, we reflect sadly, "This was not my life." In reality, we cannot be someone else. "Never try to teach a pig to sing. It wastes your time and it just annoys the pig." Perhaps what applies to pigs also applies to humans.

We are all a composite of outside influences and we are enriched by those influences, unless they dictate who we are. Then time imposes on us the ultimate trick; we become the product of someone else's time.

In Jewish folklore Zusya goes to a sage and says, "Rabbi, I'm worried. When I die and appear before God what if God welcomes me with the words, 'Zusya, I observed the way you lived and I wish to know . . . why weren't you a great leader like Moses, a philosopher like Spinoza, a scientist like Einstein?'" (In the 1990s substitute Michael Jordan, Paul Newman, Michael Jackson?) Zusya pauses. "Well, Rabbi, how will I answer?" The rabbi responds. "God, will not ask you why you weren't a Moses, a Spinoza, an Einstein. God will only ask, 'Why weren't you Zusya?'"

An African proverb says, "It is not what I call you, it is what you answer to: but if you don't know who you are anyone can name you. If anybody can name you, you will answer to anything." What names would you answer to? What percentage of your time has been devoted to what others expected of you and still expect of you? A wise grandmother asked, "If I will be she, who will be me?" When will you be you instead of he or she?

To be more yourself involves being honest with yourself. Who do you really want to be? What feels right?

Recently a play entitled *Scenes from an Execution* was performed in a small off-Broadway theater. Set in Venice shortly after the Venetian Navy defeated the Ottoman Turks, an artist Galactia is commissioned by the doge to paint the battle. The doge wants Galactia to glorify the war and celebrate Venice, but all Galactia sees is the horror of war. She paints what she sees and both government and church are aghast. Galactia cannot help herself. She must paint the truth. The play extends far beyond the indictment of war. Even beyond the realm of art. The real question is the timeless struggle between painting the truth and painting what society or family want to see. To whom do you owe ultimate loyalty in the landscape of your own life?

How have you felt when you knew you should resist external opinions, but could not? Albert Einstein concluded, "Few is the number of those who think with their own minds and feel with their own hearts." At any age.

Be yourself. Then each year will belong to you.

A Palm Branch and a Cellular Phone

Look Vertical

O N PALM SUNDAY THOUSANDS OF PILGRIMS, reenacting the drama of Jesus' entry into Jerusalem, wound their way down the bleached gravel path from Bethany to the stark Crusader Church of St. Anne tucked inside the walls of the Old City. A helicopter hovered overhead. Leaning out of the aircraft a camera crew filmed the ritual for Israeli television, French television and CNN. Beneath the helicopter Israeli soldiers carrying Uzi machine guns scampered over roof tops. Occasionally hymns were drowned out by sirens of army jeeps. Peace still loomed in the distance.

Jerusalem, in the grip of a hamsin (warm desert winds), had taken on a grey veil. Only the golden dome of the Mosque of Omar brightened the eerie atmosphere. But weather could not deter the observance of this holy day. Arab scouts from Bethlehem, Nazareth, and Hebron led the procession from Bethany. Behind the scouts, men in black and white headdress and khaki uniforms, similar to the dress worn by the fabled Arab Legion, marched with the pride of a reborn Palestinian entity. At any moment I expected to see Lawrence of Arabia charging on camel or Field Marshal Rommel in a German halftrack. Instead, a Benedictine monk, his brown cossack sweeping along the rough pavement, led a group of Italian tourists singing the "Ave Maria." The sound floated toward the Judaean Hills where shepherd boys grazed their flocks.

Pilgrims from around the world had saved for a lifetime to follow in the footsteps of Jesus. Africans chanted gospel hymns in Swahili; Japanese women in gay kimonos tread carefully on the stones and Southern Baptists from the United States cried out "Hallelujah!" The festivities reached a peak when the echo of mahogany scepters on the pavement announced the archbishop of Jerusalem, his hands raised in blessing.

Many of the spectators carried palm shoots sold by children for a dollar, but these twigs were dwarfed by a throng of Greek Orthodox waving giant fronds. My companion, Alex, the son of a Lutheran minister, nodded his approval. "Like the days of Jesus, entering Jerusalem with palm branches." Suddenly he grimaced.

"Look there," he said, pointing to a man with a black handlebar mustache, towering above his Greek coreligionists. The man's left hand carried a palm branch but his right arm was also raised. To his ear. He was speaking on a cellular phone, shouting to be heard above the chorus of "Kyrie, Kyrie."

"Who is he speaking to?" My Lutheran friend asked.

I shrugged. "His wife? Telling her when he will be home for dinner? A friend? Talking about the soccer game after the procession? Maybe he's working out a deal to sell tomatoes in Jordan."

Alex frowned. "You're probably right. This should be a day of hope, a resurrection of the spirit, but we live with the cellular phone instead of the palm branch."

Alex paused. "Sorry. I'm sounding too much like my father, but unless we rise above earthly concerns we lose the gift of the spirit." That was the message of Palm Sunday in Jerusalem.

Palm Sunday is not my religious tradition. I was only a spectator on that day in Jerusalem but I appreciate any religion that, if only for a moment, assists us in transcending earthly concerns. Why couldn't that pilgrim in Jerusalem loosen his grasp on this world? Why can't any of us? There are many ways, besides religion, to rise above mundane existence: Listen to a symphony; watch the sun shimmer on autumn leaves; read a poem that touches a hidden chord. This world is too much with us. Our days consist of work (often prosaic), car pooling, taking out the garbage, grocery shopping, and so on. Necessary activities. But every day treat yourself to an experience that touches on the spiritual. The psalmist said we were created little lower than the angels. We were granted the gift to be more than the animals, yet we seldom act upon our higher nature. That was the opportunity granted to the Palm Sunday pilgrim, an opportunity that passed him by. What have you done that elevates your day?

Watching the pilgrim with his cellular phone I remembered a Sunday morning, in Rye, New York, far away from Jerusalem. I entered the sanctuary of my temple and spotted a red phone resting on the pulpit. On a whim I picked up the receiver. Maybe, just maybe, this was a direct line to God! Every rabbi's wish! The phone was dead. Hoping that no one was observing my movements I followed the telephone wire along the floor of the sanctuary. It led to a pulpit on the far side where it connected to a blue phone. Further investigation revealed that the two phones had been used in a Sunday School skit.

I have never found a direct line to God, dreams, the richness of life. But I am certain that if that line exists it is not found between red and blue plastic phones or in the omnipresent cellular phone. They only make our world more mundane; entrap us in the mire of details, plans, minutiae.

The author of the book of Ecclesiastes wrote, "There is nothing new under the sun." In that comment he encapsulated the curse of boredom that has existed since earliest times. "There is nothing new under the sun" but there is a vast distance between earth and sun. Plan your day in a manner that lifts you above the everyday routines. Dream. Sing. Pray. Thrill to the beauty of nature.

Symbolically, all of us spend our years juxtaposed between the palm branch, waving in the heavens, and the cellular phone, our communication with this world. Life consists of a balance between the horizontal and the vertical.

Have you maintained that balance?

Are You Ahmed or Mahmoud?

Follow a Dream

HOW LONG DO YOU FOLLOW A DREAM?

I sat with the Bedouin, Mahmoud, by his campfire in the Sinai desert. Bedouins sit, actually squat, for hours without moving, at one with the unchanging pace of the desert. Mahmoud told me that once his life was different, "Let me tell you about my son, Ahmed," Mahmoud began, as he watched brown bubbles surface on pita bread baking over hot stones. He leaned against a camel saddle decorated with a coarsely woven red blanket.

"It was many years ago—when Ahmed was young. Then we lived at the oasis of Wadi Firan where Nebi Musa, your prophet Moses, had lived. Early one morning, when even the camels slept, Ahmed came to me and said, 'Father?'

'Yes, my son.'

'Father, I have seen the sun rise.'

"I looked at this boy of few years. 'Ahmed, you speak foolishness. Each morning the sun rises.'

"'I know father,' he answered, 'but it was there, just beyond the palm trees at the edge of the oasis. Tomorrow will you go with me to the place where the sun awakens?.'

"'Ahmed, the sun awakens far beyond our oasis. The light looks near but is really far away. Beyond the horizon.'

"'The horizon?'

"'Where the sky meets the earth.'

"I could not convince Ahmed.

"'Please father. Tomorrow we will meet the sun beyond the palm trees.'

"How could I refuse my son? Early the next morning we traveled to the farthest palm tree. Of course the sun did not live there. I tried to comfort Ahmed. 'No man has reached the place where the sun awakens. I am sorry my son.'

"Ahmed insisted. 'It is not here but now I know—look, the sun lies just behind those dunes. There.' And he pointed towards the south."

Mahmoud turned over the crackling pita bread.

"I promised Ahmed I would follow him behind the dunes. We packed flour to bake bread, stored water for the journey, and set out. After many hours we reached the dunes and slept. In the morning the sun was nowhere to be found. I pitied my boy who had sought the sun and found only the truth, but he did not need pity. Now he was convinced the sun hid behind the monastery of St. Katherine. We went there. Then we continued on to the sea."

A donkey brayed in the distance.

"At the sea I said, 'Ahmed I cannot go further. Come back with me to our place by the campfire. You will never reach the sun. Let us go home.'

"That is when we parted. Ahmed sailed across the sea, following the sun, for that was his dream."

I waited before asking, "And today, Mahmoud? Where is Ahmed today?"

In reply Mahmoud pulled a torn postcard from the folds of his robe. "Here, far away. Sailing on some distant sea. Still seeking the sun. And I? I stay here to watch the camels. Maybe some day, when Ahmed circles the earth, he will return to the Sinai, but who knows what drives the camel or his rider?"

Sparks from the fire escaped into the sky. Following their flight Ahmed asked, "Who is right? My son, following his dream? Myself, accepting the lot given by Allah? Who is right?"

We pondered this question until we fell asleep under the stars.

To this day I imagine that old Bedouin squatting, an immovable object at one with the desert. Methodically he turns the ashes in his fire where a blackened finjan of tea hisses softly. And far away the Bedouin's son continues on his quest to reach the horizon. Mahmoud and Ahmed, representatives of opposite approaches to life; one stagnant, trapped in time and place, the other always following a dream. "Who is right?" Mahmoud asked on that night when I slept with him under the stars. Probably neither. We need the set patterns that determine our days but we also need the dreams; otherwise, we watch our years drift away while we squat in the sands of time. When the balance between dream and routine shifts, usually dreams suffer. Especially when we age. "Dreams are for the young," a friend advised. I disagreed. "If we dream we remain young." Robert Browning counseled, "'Tis not what man does which exalts him, but what man would do."

What is the worth of life without dreams? They are the antidotes to the habits, the daily routines that consume our lives. In an interesting study of the concentration camps, two groups of inmates proved best able to surmount the dehumanizing acts of the Nazis: Zionists and Orthodox Jews. The Zionists dreamed of eventually going to the land of Israel; the Orthodox Jews rose above the horrors of this earth in their belief that there was something beyond. Without dreams, life can be a nightmare.

The story is told of a baby eagle who was raised with a flock of chickens. Day after day the eagle followed the chickens foraging for seeds in the farmer's yard, fleeing from the occasional fox, and hiding in the far corner of the coop. The eagle had developed into a model chicken until, one day, the farmer took the eagle to a high cliff towering above the plains and released the bird. At first the traumatized eagle sank. Then suddenly it spread its wings, caught an air current, and flew into the heavens.

Some of us never recognize that we are eagles with the ability to soar.

Every afternoon two women walk past my house. One takes sure strides, her head raised. The other walks with head lowered to the ground. Two types of people: one attuned to what is above and beyond, the other unable to see beyond her own feet. What kind of person are you? When did you last have a dream that you attempted or planned to attempt? Yesterday? I hope so.

It is easy to become sedentary, to offer excuses for why we should not follow our dream. "It's the wrong timing?" "At my age?" "I'm a mature person." "Can I afford it?" "I'm not the adventurous kind," "Life is a serious business," "I've always considered myself practical." The list is endless.

We build our lives on rationalizations, reasons why we cannot instead of reasons why we can. I am not a stranger to this process. One summer, vacationing in Provence, I found myself caught between my everyday self and my higher self. The struggle involved climbing Mount Ventoux.

Mount Ventoux dominates the northern section of Provence, proud master over a countryside covered with purple lavender. Immortalized in the fourteenth century by Petrarch, who described his climb to the summit, six thousand and three hundred feet high, Ventoux towers over the towns of Malemorte, Vaison La Romaine, Brantes, Bedoin.

The mountain exists to be climbed and Marion and I knew we could not leave France without attempting the ascent, but each day passed with another excuse. "Do we want to leave our chateau in the vineyard to hike in a maze of black pine?" "Will we find the way?" "How treacherous is the peak over loose shale?" "Why risk a climb when clouds might obscure the view?" "Will Marion survive twenty-three hairpin turns in the descent by bus?" When a person seeks excuses they pop up from every corner. Finally we concluded: "Maybe next trip," and to justify our decision I added: "Reality never equals the dream. We would only be disappointed."

However, several days before our departure from France, the tourist office in Bedoin advertised: "Guided Tour up Mt. Ventoux. Friday evening, June 21, celebrate the fete of St. Jean, the longest day of the year. Giant bonfire at summit." Thirty seconds later we had paid our fifty francs and were committed to the climb. Sitting in the town square with a bottle of wine and a piece of chevre we read about the trek. Climbing Mount Ventoux was classified as an extremely difficult climb. I finished the bottle of wine, ordered a second and tried to forget about our rash decision.

On the day of the climb the sky was painted dark blue, but a fierce mistral wind had rushed across Provence. "Parkas and ski pants advised." We had shorts and T-shirts. A group of women hikers in dresses and high heel shoes gathered at the starting point. An encouraging sign. The trail must be easy. Five minutes before departure they vanished into the trunk of their Peugeot and reemerged in hiking pants and leather boots, sinewy muscles quivering. From mortals to superwomen! The hour was 5:00 P.M. when we noticed a small sign on the bulletin board in the tourist office. "Slow hikers should begin the ascent of Mt. Ventoux at 3:00 P.M." Seeking reassurance we asked the guide, a French World War II veteran with short-cropped hair, "Is the trail dangerous?" He smiled and answered "Oui! Oui!" (Later we discovered our guide did not speak English.) A French TV crew followed. The French love horror movies. Was the crew along to film a nail-biting feature, *Death at 6.300*? Marion noticed I had taken on the color of Mount Ventoux's summit. Gray. "Say something," she implored. In the spirit of Petrarch I recited the poetry of Langston Hughes. "What happens to a dream deferred—does it dry up like a raisin in the sun?"

"Let's see what happens to a dream deferred," I suggested, "and get out of here." Too late. We were on our way and the French TV cameraman had his camera and jet black beard in our faces. "And now! Les Americains." Or something similar. "Monsieur and Mesdames is this hike difficult?" Marion responded. "Compared to living in New York?"

Buoyed by our comparison to New York we proceeded briskly until Marion asked, "How much further?" Unfortunately we did not understand the French reply. "A little?" "Some?" "Most of the way?" Never ask how far away a dream. Or, in the words of Nike, "Just do it."

In four hours we had emerged from the woods and there, looming above our heads, the dramatic peak of Mount Ventoux crowned by a massive pyramid shaped radar station burst out of the shadows. Day was departing and I identified Marseilles off in the distance, the Mediterranean, the Rhone Valley, the High Alps. Night moved in, tucking the scene into its widespread arms. We sought warmth inside a fourteenth century chapel.

At 10:30 P.M. a giant bonfire leapt into the sky and a bearded elder read his homage to the day when the sun lingered. Gnarled grape vines fed the fire, macabre shapes glowing a brilliant red, and French TV approached for their final interview with Les Americains.

"Why did you climb Mount Ventoux?"

Marion, our resident French linguist, answered: "My dream. Since coming to France. My dream. To climb Mount Ventoux. And to think, I almost didn't!" On this ecstatic note the cameraman called. "Cut! Spotlights fade!"

The next day, ensconced in our vineyard below Mount Ventoux, I looked at the distant mountain, the radar station shrunk to miniature, and thought: That's the way it is with dreams. They only last the moment! But what a magnificent moment—one in which I stood on a level with the setting sun and saw the distant corners of our world. Darkness may embrace the valleys but, for those willing to climb the mountain, a bonfire lights the way. At least once, everyone should climb a mountain and fulfill a dream. Then the ruts below will disappear from view.

PART 4

THE ATM AND THE HOURGLASS

Outwitting Time

The ATM and the Hourglass

Outwitting Time

I NEVER USE AN ATM. WHEN I ENTER CITIBANK on Main Street in Armonk, New York, I walk quickly past the ATM and approach the counter. My son has tried to convince me that an ATM is more efficient but he doesn't understand; I go into the bank to play with an hourglass that sits on the counter next to the teller's window. Since I began banking at Citibank a multicolored hourglass occupies a prominent position next to printed matter advertising mortgage rates, investment advice, and a customer service phone. The present hourglass consists of a plastic cube containing colored liquid. When the cube turns over a drop of blue liquid descends a circuitous route until it reaches the bottom, followed by a second, a third, a fourth drop until all the water lies on the bottom. The time involved is less than an hour. Everything occurs faster in the 1990s.

Why does Citibank display this modified hourglass? To demonstrate that time is money? To encourage customers to invest in the future? No. The answer is quite simple. To amuse me. Whenever I stand in line I flip over the cube before the water completes its descent. If the line is too long I leave my place and barge to the front to complete my mission before the last drip drops. I have acquired quite a reputation at Citibank. The tellers smile when I rush the counters; the customers gasp. Never mind.

At first my obsession with the Citibank hourglass was a frivolous pursuit but, in recent years, flipping the glass has become a serious challenge. The bottom line? I want to stop time from running out. Trick time. When I am on the scene the liquid on the top never lies exhausted on the bottom. Before time runs out I am there to flip over the cube and reverse the flow. Sometimes I actually stop a drop in its track, and Geraldine (the present keeper of the glass) considers me a local folk hero. Since I cannot be on the scene from 8:00 A.M. to 5:00 P.M. (Citibanking hours) I have considered deputizing a cadre of Armonk residents to stand in line and turn over the hourglass. I even considered enlisting the homeless for this task but Bob, manager of Citibank, vetoed this proposal. So it's just me—and anyone who, after reading this plea, volunteers to take a shift.

I know the futility of my project. Time cannot be stopped. I may flip over the glass before time runs out, but in the world beyond Citibank? Impossible. We cannot stop time at the joyous moments of life, hasten time at sad moments. We cannot flip the years and begin again. I cannot vanish into a phone booth, emerge dressed like an hourglass, and save endangered time with the flip of a hand. I cannot gain extra time. The hours will exhaust themselves; one day remaining one day. I may trick the hourglass, but outwitting time presents a formidable challenge.

However, I refuse to admit defeat. Certain techniques, described in the following pages, permit us to symbolically stretch time. Unlike the hourglass, we don't have to wait for someone to turn us over. We can create methods to enhance each day, achieve a higher interest rate on our investment in time—and never use the ATM.

The Peddler of Junk

Don't Throw Away Time

T WICE A YEAR MR. MARTIN, THE PEDDLER, came to our house on South Main Avenue. The peddler possessed an exquisite sense of timing, arriving when junk poured out of every closet. Miraculously, Mr. Martin would appear at the back screen door, usually when my mother was baking an apple pie, and his greeting filtered through the wire mesh. "Hello Ma'am, any junk for Mr. Martin?" Out tumbled chipped dishes, a rusty knife, my purple panda (the one missing a right eye and a left foot), the spare tire from the Plymouth that broke down on State Street Hill and sat at Armory Used Cars with the sign "Almost Good As New." (Mr. Martin didn't deal in cars.) The peddler stuffed our family heirlooms in a torn black canvas duffel, paid us with a "Thanks" (in those days we didn't think to ask for a receipt for tax purposes), and headed down South Main.

My father never met Mr. Martin until one hot summer's day when Dad came home early. Near our house Dad passed the wizened little peddler who wore a tweed jacket with a leather patch on one elbow and a fishing cap with two hooks still embedded in the brim. (The hat dated to Mr. Jaffee's 1947 fishing expedition in Alaska). Dad, always a friendly man, said "Hello," and Mr. Martin, eyeing my father's tattered briefcase, a future addition to his collectibles, wiped his brow and returned the greeting. Soon my father discovered that this was the legendary Mr. Martin who appeared mysteriously from unknown climes. "My wife speaks of you with awe," Dad exclaimed. Mr. Martin, encouraged by this warm reception, spread his acquisitions on the lawn next to Mr. Jaffee's marigold bed. Rummaging through the pile of throwaways Dad spotted a rectangular Elgin watch with a broken glass face. He tried on the cracked leather watchband. Turning to the peddler he asked:

"What can I give you for this watch? A real heirloom."

Mr. Martin answered, "I only sell in flea markets," stuffed his belongings back into the duffel and picked a marigold for his button hole. Looking up the peddler continued, "Also, this watch, I might keep it. Lost one like it last year. Fishing. But . . ." Mr. Martin, hesitated. "I see you appreciate fine Jewelry—for $5.75 its yours."

Delighted with his acquisition my father rushed home to show my mother. "Dear, only $5.75. I bought this from that peddler you talk about. Mr. Martin. A charming man with fine merchandise."

My mother shuddered. "Sam, I gave that watch to Mr. Martin. That was your old Elgin. The one you haven't worn in years."

According to family lore, my father put the watch back into the drawer of his Hitchcock dresser under a sweater he also didn't wear. When Mother told the story Dad always added, "I don't have any regrets about buying that watch, even if I never used it. How can you throw away time? My wife can throw away everything I have—except time. There's never enough of that."

My father died one year later at the age of fifty-eight.

Did my father intuit his approaching death? Was that the symbolism behind buying his old watch? Probably not. My father understood the precious quality of time. Retrieving that watch was a whimsical way of saying to time: "You are mine, to shape, to fashion as I wish. I will not throw you away. I may only have 58 years to live but those years will be mine.

Henry David Thoreau, observing nature by Walden Pond, reflected, "Time is but the stream I go a fishing in. I drink at it but while I drink I see the sandy bottom and detect how shallow it is." This year I am 58, the same age as my father when he died and the sandy bottom looms especially close. Until now I believed I would live forever—a normal and healthy response. How many of us wish to confront our own mortality? But occasionally, in recent days, I have reminded myself: "You are fifty-eight, Dan, the same age as your father was when he died. The depth of years may be shallow," and now, when I fish, I attempt to cast my lines in pools and eddys that work for me. We have two choices. The first, to be driven by time like a leaf floating on a gust of wind. The alternative is to shape our lives in such a way that, although the length of years remains unknown, we use time fully and in a way that satisfies us. This approach enables us to outsmart time.

For example, I am a telescope addict. The kind of addict who cannot resist looking through a telescope at an observation point. At the top of the Shilthorn Mountain in Switzerland (made famous when James Bond skied down its slope in the movie *On Her Majesty's Secret Service*) a revolving telescope focused on the Jungfrau, Mount Blanc, the Dolomites. After inserting a Swiss franc into the slot I scanned the dazzling panorama of snow capped peaks until time ran out and the shutter dropped over the lens. As I stepped away a Frenchman took my place but, with time still on his telescope, left the stand. How could he leave before his time ran out? As a telescope fundamentalist I watched in horror. Quickly I remounted the stand in time for one more view of the Eiger.

How do we let time slip by, the shutter closing without using our allotment? One way is to fail to look at the panorama time provides. The night of the meteor shower I fell asleep before the galaxy exploded. The day of the Bach Cantata I decided not to make the effort to drive into New York City and, on the crisp January day when the cross-country trail lay under a layer of fresh snow, I lacked the incentive to rise from the couch. Time slipped by, carrying wondrous moments, and I watched it depart.

Yesterday the Hammacher Schlemmer holiday catalog "Offering the Best, the Only and the Unexpected for over 148 Years," arrived at my house. For $43,000 I can buy an authentic London Taxi Cab, for $399.95 a Galileo's Liquid Thermometer, an F-16 Flight Training Simulator, a correct posture Dog Feeder, recommended by veterinarians to maintain a dog's proper muscular and skeletal alignment while eating, and a Dancing Elvis Presley telephone. Where else can anyone buy these necessities of life? Only at Hammacher Schlemmer. But with regret I announce, Hammacher Schlemmer is not selling time for the holidays. I don't know whether they ran out or whether their supplier failed, but for whatever the reason you cannot buy time from Hammacher Schlemmer, the store with everything. Sorry.

In the marketplace we often refer to time as money. Time is not money. Time is life but life can be spent in frivolous ways or productive ways. And, unlike money, time cannot be saved, it cannot be recycled and it will not gather interest. What happened to your yesterday? What is happening to your today? Are they being used well? No one can define how you spend time, but periodically you might sit back and evaluate who is ahead in the challenge match between you and time. If you conclude that you have been drifting in your life then time is ahead. If you conclude that much of your life has been shaped in ways you have chosen then you are ahead. To prepare for what might be a harsh evaluation remember the words of the first century Roman philosopher Seneca: "We are always complaining that our days are few, and acting as though there would be no end to them." We are so fond of life—and so careless of life.

Time can be an adversary vanishing from before your grasp because you did not reach out. Time can also be a companion inviting you to fulfill the span of your years. To shape time to your advantage, the next time you glance at your watch you might promise, "I won't throw you away."

The Twenty-five Hour Day

How to Stretch Time

NOT LONG AGO I OFFICIATED AT AN especially poignant wedding. It began with a telephone call.

"Rabbi, Chris and I want to be married."

"Wonderful," I answered.

Marie had been alone for many years, raising two sons who were now teenagers, and I was happy she had found a partner, but on this gray October day there was a trace of melancholy in her voice.

"When is the wedding date?" I asked.

"Sunday."

"Sunday?" I echoed. "This Sunday?"

A nervous laugh. "Yes, this Sunday. I know it's short notice. I'll understand if you aren't free."

"You need a license, and today's Friday." To lighten the atmosphere I added, "And a wedding dress, and a photographer, and a caterer, and, and, and."

"Rabbi," Marie interrupted, "I did that at my first marriage and now, now we don't have much time. Chris has been diagnosed with a rare blood disease. The doctors don't know how long. . . ." Her voice trailed off. "But we want to say 'I take you, in good fortune or in adversity.' We want to be one before we are apart." In a whisper she asked, "Can you? Will you? Please."

"Tell me where, Marie. And what time. Of course I'll be there."

Early Sunday morning I found myself heading north on the Taconic Parkway. Deer grazed by the side of the road. Overhead wisps of clouds punctuated the blue sky, a precursor of Hurricane Edward racing up the eastern seaboard. Driving, I wondered what I could say to this handsome couple, determined to harvest every moment. I checked the hour on the dashboard clock. 10:30 A.M. I was late! The wedding was scheduled for 11:00 A.M. Where was I? Todd Hill Road. Even if I averaged 65 MPH I was still an hour away. Then I remembered I had forgotten to turn back the clock early that morning when we had changed to Eastern Standard Time. It was only 9:30. I breathed a sigh of relief as I passed a field of pumpkins ripening on the vine—and suddenly I knew what I would say to Marie and Chris as they exchanged vows in the courtyard of the country inn beneath a canopy of wild grasses braided with blue and red asters, pink cosmos, and field daisies.

"Marie and Chris you have promised to share whatever the future holds." Chris stood proudly in his blue blazer and white slacks as Marie, dressed in a pink suit, a single red rose highlighting her blonde hair, looked at him with adoration. "Moments of joy will be even greater because you smile and you laugh as one and the inevitable moments of unrest less intense because, as you hold one another's hand at this moment, so you will hold one another's life."

Family wept openly. Tears of happiness. "Finally, they are husband and wife. Finally." Tears of sadness. "But tomorrow. What of tomorrow?"

My words resounded in the chill October weather.

"Marie, when you called and expressed the wish to be married today I thought, 'so soon, so soon,' but this morning I understood. Today is the longest day of the year. A perfect day to be married." Marie and Chris looked at one another. Puzzled. "I know, usually we think of June 21st as the longest day, not October 28th but last night those of us who remembered turned our clocks back, and we gained an extra hour. This is the only day when we have twenty-five hours." Chris smiled. With the bitter-sweet destiny of this couple as a backdrop I continued:

"It would be my prayer that every day will be the longest day of the year for you; measured not by hours but by the fullness of joy, of happiness and of fulfillment. May you vow to stretch the hours between sunrise and sunset as if they were endless. That is my wish for you on this, the longest day of the year, and the first day of your life together."

As Marie and Chris shared champagne toasts I wandered down a steep path leading to a pasture where a newly born colt on spindly legs awkwardly tested life and I thought: Some of us are granted long years. Extra hours. Others find life seized away prematurely. But we can live each day as if it will never end. Stretch out each day. Then, when it is time to say good bye, we will look back and with contentment say, "I lived each day as if it were the longest day of the year; each moment complete, each breath treasured. For that gift I am deeply thankful."

A twenty-five hour day comes once a year. Only wishful thinking would create an extra hour everyday; that is a trick time will not permit. But we can stretch a day by fully appreciating the time we have. Why do we wait for a warning crisis? Why do we wait for a loved one to have breast cancer, a debilitating accident, the death of a child to understand the value of what we have. Edna St. Vincent Millay cried out "O world, I cannot hold thee close enough!" The great gift is to hold those we love tightly, to savor the fullness of life, not after we have suffered but in the midst of sunlight. That is how we stretch time; by reaping the bounty of each hour before it is too late. Don't praise a friend or family member in a eulogy after they have died. Appreciate them fully while they are alive and tell them of your feelings. Perhaps eulogies should be for the living!

How do we maximize our time? Trick time? Avoid losing precious days? By loving those close to us even more. By becoming more aware of our lives and the lives of others. By acknowledging and acting on the wisdom that life is too brief to be petty.

If we counted the meaningless rifts we have had with families and with friends, they would probably add up to more than we wish to acknowledge. And what was accomplished? If only we could regain the hours wasted by our own neglect. Once a year we can add one hour. 365 times a year we can add richness to each day.

In her later years Colette mused, "What a wonderful life I've had. I only wish I'd realized it sooner." But how many of us do? Even if we were granted extra hours, would we grasp their value or would they slip away like sand being washed out to sea? Time fools us by encouraging us to believe we have forever and can waste time as though we had a million years.

On a morning when pumpkins ripened on the vine, a morning inaugurating a 25-hour day, Chris and Marie took their vows in the courtyard of a country inn. When they repeated, "I do," they meant far more than "I do take you to be my husband, my wife." The voices that floated across the meadows echoed a second vow. "I do intend to make each day as full as possible, to stretch the quality of time. Until death do us part."

The earlier we make that vow, the longer the span of our lives.

There Is No Finish Line

After Every Ending—Begin Again

S USAN'S HAND SHOOK AS SHE GRIPPED the Number 2 pencil. Slowly she drew a heavy black line through "Have water on the pulpit," the last item on her yellow sheet. Bruce, Susan's husband, popped open a bottle of champagne and a cheer filled the sanctuary. "Congratulations, Susan! You did it!"

What Susan had done, on the eve of her son Scott's Bar Mitzvah, was to complete the list of "Must Do's." For months, even years, Susan had never been seen without yellow legal pads overflowing with notes on the momentous event. Next week the folio of crossed out pads would be bound in a leather cover and placed on the coffee table of the den next to a video of the service, the album from the society photographer, "Now We Are 13," and a collage of valium prescriptions tenderly saved by Bruce.

For those who may not visit Susan and Bruce's home I have been given permission to share highlights of the sheets, some stained by age.

Page 1. March 7, 1983. Scott: Age 1 1/2

1. Ask pediatrician why Scott cannot speak English; a prerequisite for admission to the Temple's Hebrew School.
2. Ask Temple whether age 3 is too old to begin Hebrew.

3. Inquire about weather condition for Scott's Bar Mitzvah on Saturday, April 3, 1995.
4. Find tutor to help Bruce and myself with toast at Bar Mitzvah party.
etc. etc. etc.

We skip to 1991.

Page 47. January 14, 1991

1. Call Jason's mother and tell her to change Jason's Bar Mitzvah. That's Scott's date
2. Hire band.
3. Hire caterer.
4. Buy second case of yellow pads.
5. Check weather update for April 3, 1995.

Page 176. April 1, 1995

1. Remind band to play "You are the sunshine of my life."
2. Tell Scott to quit growing. He's too tall for his suit.
3. Buy boutonnieres.
4. Take Kleenex to temple.
etc. etc. etc.

After thirteen and a half years in progress, the book with the stirring title, *Lists for Scott's Bar Mitzvah,* was complete. Instead of rejoicing, Susan left the champagne party bubbling over in the last row of the sanctuary and slipped into my office. "Rabbi, I'm depressed. Now that everything's complete the Bar Mitzvah seems anticlimactic. And I don't know what to do without a yellow pad in my hand. Since Scott's birth I was never without a pad. I had one next to my bed at night, another in a plastic cover taped to the side of the jacuzzi. In my car I stopped to write down notes. Once I even came to a dead stop in the passing lane of the New York Thruway. What of my future?"

I smiled. "Susan, your reaction is quite common. You are entering PBMS, post Bar Mitzvah syndrome, a common malaise affecting women at your stage of life. Monday at 11:00 you can join our support group and share this experience with other mothers."

Susan shook her head, uncertain of both diagnosis and cure.

"However," I continued, "before the Bar Mitzvah we still have practical considerations. For instance, who are your ushers tomorrow? We need three."

Susan gasped: "Oh God," she cried. "You didn't tell me." Her face brightened. 'Where is my yellow pad?" Searching through her leather pocket book she pulled out a yellow pad, then muttered.

"This is the wrong pad." Scrawled on the cover were the words. "Lists for Scott's wedding."

1. Remind Scott to save the first dance for me.
2. Tell Scott he cannot marry anyone unless Scott and his wife have Thanksgiving with *his* family. Etc. etc. etc.

Pronounced breaks in time constitute lost time. Although we need to refresh ourselves periodically, we always need something to look forward to. In the words of Nike, "There is no finish line." At the end of the Jewish High Holy Days (equal to Christmas for Christian clergy, April 15 for accountants, the NCAA basketball finals for the University of North Carolina) a heavy burden slides off my shoulders. The first night of release I skip through my house whistling and shouting, "Free at last, free at last, thank God almighty I'm free at last" (with apologies to Martin Luther King). But, by the next morning I am restless. Nothing to do. I am losing time instead of gaining time.

Oliver Wendell Holmes understood this phenomenon: "The racers do not stop short when they reach the goal. There is a little finishing canter before coming to a standstill—the race is over, but the work is never done while the power to work remains. For to live is to function. That is all there is to living."

How do you feel when you complete a project? A momentary high? And then? Make your life a series of beginnings. Even as you appreciate today plan for tomorrow.

A friend of mine is a prolific writer. Every morning, from 7:00 A.M. to 11:00 A.M. he works on his book and, from 1:00 P.M. to 4:00 P.M. he researches his next book. The day he hands in his finished work he is off and writing. He lives for today and plans for tomorrow.

In Judaism, at the conclusion of the Day of Atonement, we hammer in the first nail for the Succah, the tabernacle symbolizing the coming holiday of Succoth and commemorating the Israelites' desert dwellings. Nothing ends unless something else begins. Boredom evolves from not doing.

On a recent trip to Israel I visited an Iranian Jew named Yoav. On his farm he grew fig trees. One tree seemed to measure two-hundred feet across. Closer examination revealed that Yoav had overlapped the branches. There were twenty trunks.

Time can also be interconnected, one aspect leading into the next.

One of the sadder epochs in my family history concerns a family heirloom, a grandfather clock. The story began at 11:00 A.M. on my mother's eighty-sixth birthday. That was when time stopped. Time represented by a grandfather clock acquired by my father in 1923 when he graduated from rabbinical seminary and moved to Boston.

No one knew the exact age of the clock with the gray schooner painted on the pendulum's glass cover, but it has spent many years with our family, traveling to Wilkes Barre, Pennsylvania, Albany, New York and, now, to my home in Mount Kisco.

The clock was rather laid-back. It just did its thing. With one exception: It insisted on being wound every seven days, although technically it was an eight-day clock. Respecting the clocks penchant for time we wound the mechanism ritually on the seventh day.

Until Grace arrived. Grace, hired as a caretaker for my mother, entered our family's history in the 1980s when mother lived in a small apartment on South Allen Street in Albany.

Grace's bed was situated under the grandfather clock. Faithfully the clock bonged away the half-hour and the hour, reaching a crescendo at 12:00 when twelve mighty bongs filled the apartment, awakening Grace from a deep sleep. With admiration I noted that even at one hundred years of age the clock displayed the vigor of its youth. Grace was not impressed and issued a declaration known in family history as "The Ultimatum of Grace." Condensed to a single sentence: "Either I go or the clock goes!" Reluctantly I explained to the clock that this was one time when we needed Grace more than we needed the correct time. Sadly, on my mother's eighty-sixth birthday I performed a pendulumectomy. At 11:00 A.M. on that doleful morning, the clock ceased one hundred years of loyal beating. A year later my mother's heart also wound down and stopped beating.

After Mother's death I brought the clock to the living room of our farmhouse in Mount Kisco and rewound the family heirloom. I could almost hear the sailors in the painting of the schooner sigh as the steady rhythm of the pendulum again lulled them to sleep. However, the clock lost time and on day four, without warning, the pendulum fell silent. Further attempts to breathe life into the clock failed. The hour was 11:00 A.M.

Perhaps the clock chose 11:00 in memory of my mother or perhaps as a protest against my attempt to tinker with time. Someday I will find a repair man to revive the clock for another hundred years, because I am troubled with the thought that time has stopped. People die. That is inevitable. Not only people, but dreams, loves, hopes for the future. But time moves on, with or without us.

Who will wind the human spirit? Who can convince us to forge ahead, seizing the hands of time? Only ourselves. Do not wait for the eighth day. Wind, wind, your own mechanism and listen to the small voice. "Tick, tock. Tick, tock." "Get on with life. Get on with life."

Your clock will cease, probably before you are ready, but never arbitrarily stop the hands of time—or your place on those hands of time.

The Painter of Montbrun

Live and Paint Slowly

F OR FIVE DAYS I WATCHED A PAINTER supported by wooden crutches swing along the street of Montbrun Les Bains. At La Chochinelle Supermarket, the insignia of a red ladybug sketched on the awning, the old man opened his easel, spread out his paints and studied a partially finished canvas. It was late May but the wind whistled off Mount Ventoux and the painter pulled his brown fedora tightly over his head. The hat barely covered silver hair cascading down his neck.

The artist played with the creative colors of his imagination then, dipping into the chaos of bright pigments on his palette, he placed a brilliant red on the canvas and the image of the Pharmacie des Thermes, opposite La Cochinelle, emerged. Not the Pharmacie today; the Pharmacie in an earlier era. In the painting, peach colored walls took on a deeper tone and shutters sparkled with lavender hues. Window boxes emerged and a woman dressed in a white robe watered geraniums and laughed while speaking with her next door neighbor. Beneath a canopy of red, white, and blue French flags a trumpeter with a red cap and a yellow trumpet gathered the people together to announce the Bastille Day celebration. A fire cart emerged beside the Pharmacie and the painter's brush flashed from palette to painting. The turn of the century town of Montbrun Les Bains had come alive on canvas. Townspeople gathered to watch the painter, his eyes twinkling and his voice raised in a French chanson. Imbued with the spirit of his craft, the painter waved his arms, spackling a nearby plane tree with yellow paint. Enthusiastically he interpreted his work. "A century ago, before radio, newspapers, television, the town trumpeter would stand here. Yes, Girard, right where you stand now, in front of the Pharmacie des Thermes, and with a blast of the trumpet would announce the news."

Every day the artist assembled his audience. Young Pierre, kicking a soccer ball, stopped for a brief lecture on art; the butcher, carrying a string of sausages, chatted with the old man; Swiss backpackers rested their heavy packs on the hood of a gray Citroen and listened to the story of the painter's life. "I come to Montbrun from Brussels. My wife drives me to the village to paint."

His wife stood off to one side and smiled. She knew that when her husband had an audience he would not paint. On warmer days he would tip his plaid beret and beat a rhythm on the green corduroys covering his legs, but he would not paint. "He likes to talk too much, especially with the little ones, to bring them into the world on canvas. He talks instead of painting. But does he think he will live forever?" Slowly the man closed his easel, leaned on his wife's arm and they left for their chateau on the edge of Montbrun.

I was with the Belgian painter the day he completed his work. While his wife looked on with unspoken intimacy he placed his signature on the painting. The signature was not a name. His final strokes, in the lower right hand corner, sketched a tiny portrait of a painter standing at an easel. His self-portrait. How many homes and galleries would he visit in the years to come? Wherever the painting traveled, from owner to owner, home to home he would be there, joined to the work he loved.

Like many of us, the painter did not want to reach his goal—to complete the canvas. Each painting would, he hoped, continue without end; always another stroke, a tint of color to add. And, when the final stroke was placed on the canvas he painted, or the canvas of his years, he would have inserted himself into the lives of others, a small figure in the lower right hand corner. He would continue the ongoing process of a painter, his work, and his life. In the French village of Montbrun Les Bains.

The elderly painter in Montbrun had mastered the ability to slow time. Instead of rushing to his goal he said "Wait! I am not impatient to arrive. I will play with time instead of permitting time to play with me." How did the painter control time? By painting slowly, by grasping every excuse to prolong the work.

Once I drove a cancer patient to his daily treatments at Yale-New Haven Hospital. On one of those trips he related a dream. "Rabbi, last night I saw a giant hand descending from the sky and hovering over my bed. I knew what the hand wanted. This was it. The final call." Sweat broke out on his forehead. "I pushed the hand away. I yelled. 'I'm not ready! Go! Leave me!' And the hand vanished. I am going to push that hand away until the very end. How long do you think I have?" The answer was six months.

Certain endings are inevitable, but we can push them further away by lingering over the canvas of our lives. What is the hurry? In Tokyo I witnessed a tea ceremony. Slowly, deliberately, the tea master enacted each phase of the ancient rite while I sat on a straw mat. Time seemed to stop in that tea house, but, at the conclusion of the ceremony I reentered Tokyo and descended to the metro station. Huge crowds squeezed onto a train and officially designated "pushers" packed people tightly inside before the train flew through the underground caverns of Tokyo. Somewhere between tea ceremony and subway lies an appropriate compromise.

How often have you said. "It went by so fast. Our daughter's childhood, the wedding, our lives." Time always moves at the same speed but we rush the process when we fail to dabble slowly in the palette of our days, listen to the rhythm of our lives and tell the story of our lives to whomever will listen. For the painter in Montbrun every stroke was a self-contained portrait.

With the passage of time I admire that painter and his ability to slow time—but he had a second trick to outwit time. By placing himself in the corner of the canvas he could dabble in whimsy; he could imagine where he and his painting might travel. From Bastille Day, 1914, he would travel to an art gallery in Brussels in 1997, a salon in Bruges in 2001, a home in Rotterdam in 2020. In the world of imagination he could take a mystery ride wherever he desired.

A friend related a strange phone call he received. "Meet at 73rd and Park at 5:30 September 14. Dress casually." This particular individual, a logical individual who preferred the known to the mysterious, agreed but did not look forward to the evening. Fifteen couples were taken on a mystery ride for cocktails at the Temple of Dendur in the Metropolitan Museum of Art, a nighttime cruise around Manhattan Island, and dancing at a nightclub. "At first I begged my hostess to reveal our destination but eventually I settled in—what a great night!"

Do you do well with the unknown? Do you read the last page of a book first? Do you understand that life is really a mystery ride? When you appreciate the mystery of life the days lengthen. When you narrowly circumscribe your days you arrive too early. The painter of Montbrun painted himself into the corner of the canvas but not into the narrow corners of life.

Sunflower Seeds

Plant for the Future

THE WEATHER-BEATEN FRENCH FARMER and the field of drooping sunflowers resembled one another. After a golden summer the blossoms hung laconically on unsteady stalks. Shriveled petals encircled hundreds of seeds clustered in the middle of the flower. And the farmer? Slowly he eased himself along the rows, leaning on a walking stick and swinging his scythe laboriously. Sunflowers fell to his feet.

Nearing the farmer I said, "Those sunflowers. Sad. The end of the season. I wonder if they accept their fate, or if, like humans, they wish desperately to hold on to summer?" The farmer tipped a leather hat stained with sweat and replied, "Your observation, Monsieur, is not correct. This is the beginning of the season for these sunflowers." A twinkle came to his eyes and he rested against a pile of shriveled stalks. "The stalks. They are finished. They will kindle my fire. But the flowers?" He snapped off a blossom and broke the disc-shaped pod in two. "What do you see?"

"Seeds. Hundreds of sunflower seeds in a single head."

"Voila!" the farmer cried with a strength belying his years. "Voila! In the spring I planted a single seed. Now look. Many, many seeds. More seeds than I have grandchildren. And sir, I have twenty-three grandchildren." A handful of black kernels slipped through the old man's leathery hands.

Impressed with both the crop of grandchildren and sunflower seeds I asked. "What do you do with the seeds?"

"I will store the seeds. In my barn. Next spring I will plant. Each year my fields grow larger. Oh! From one, many. That is the fate of which you speak."

Retrieving his scythe he disappeared down the rows while I admired his energy. Where did he gain the strength to work the fields? From his conviction that he harvested for the future. More sunflowers. More grandchildren. The anticipation of rebirth.

Like the flowers of the field, seasons pass. There are times when we feel cut off from our roots. A season ends, a love dies, a hope burns off in the morning sun and we stumble, unsure of the future. Seeds of possibility lie dormant. What is the challenge of life? To uncover the source of new beginnings, free the spirit for a spring planting.

And, at the final harvest, if we have lived life well we will leave a legacy; not necessarily twenty-three grandchildren but ideas, stories, memories clustered together in the hearts of those who knew us; seeds for the next generation.

The cutting of a stalk in autumn anticipates springtime.

Why do we think of time as limited? Why is death an ending? In many religions death is a beginning, but for those without a belief in an afterlife we fear time will end; our place on the continuum will end—unless we act like the sunflower and sow a new life.

Judaism boasts of its own Johnny Appleseed, a man named Honi. Everyday Honi would go into the countryside and plant a seed. Passersby would scoff. "Honi, you will never live to sit under the shade of that tree or reap the fruit." Calmly Honi replied, "I plant for those who follow."

What is immortality? A victory over time. How do we achieve immortality? By planting seeds of hope, love, wisdom in the fertile soil of friend and stranger. No one can reach fruition on their own and when you plant a seed of yourself you live on and you influence others.

The View from Fourteen Thousand Feet

Focus on the Important

I HAD EASED MY WAY AROUND A ROCKY PATH, still slippery from a morning dusting of snow. If only I were a yak! Undaunted they lumbered-over the Nepalese mountain trails. But I wasn't a yak; I was only a human with Timberland boots, two blisters and a liberal coating of Moleskin. Would a yak ever come to New York City? So why was I hiking in the Himalayas? Why? Because around that last bend, where the path flattened out and the trickle of thaw formed tiny pools, a majestic white peak crowned with black rock bound heaven to earth. Mount Everest.

What a view! Mount Everest in her blanket of white—and Hiroshi, carrying a Nikon, a Leica, and a Hasselblad! Hiroshi was a professional photographer from Kyoto. When I spied him mounting his Hasselblad on a tripod I knew I had a photographic scoop. Whatever Hiroshi did, I would do. For once my photographs would come out. Tenderly I took my one touch, automatic focus, point and shoot Instamatic out of my L.L. Bean backpack. I beamed. Here I was, in the mountains of Nepal, with Hiroshi of Kyoto. Hasselblad Hiroshi and Instamatic Dan. Photographers at the top of the world.

I waited for Hiroshi to shoot but he was fiddling with the Nikon. And then I witnessed a scene of great drama unfolding in the ravine below. Three thousand feet below. Two yaks were crossing the Kosi River carrying my blue duffels. At least I think they were yaks and I think they were my duffels. I could not be certain from that distance. And there was Marion sitting on the bridge and eating rice from a bowl. Or was it the sherpa girl who brought hot tea to our tent every morning? Never mind! This was a slice of humanity worthy of my Instamatic. Steadying myself on a rock outcropping I pointed my camera and shot. Again! Again! Oh joy! Oh happiness! Oh for the wonder of a sublime photo opportunity!

Meanwhile Hiroshi, absorbed in changing the infrared lens of his Leica, was missing the drama of life unfolding just below his feet. Three thousand feet below his feet. I felt sorry for my friend. He was missing it all. Missing a yak, a duffel, a wife, a bowl of rice. Fame and fortune. The cover picture of *National Geographic*. All mine! All mine! But was it proper to gloat? Should I seize this opportunity for myself alone? Of course not! At fourteen thousand feet, immersed in Buddhist culture, I remembered my own heritage, a Jewish sage named Hillel who lived two thousand years ago and asked, "If I am for myself alone what am I?" And the Bible. Leviticus. "Do unto others as you would have them to unto you." My good side battled with my bad side and, I am proud to say, my good side won out. Hurray for the forces of good! So I nudged Hiroshi's Nikon, effectively jabbing the photographer in the side and pointed to the bridge. "See, a yak, a wife, a bowl of rice. A picture!"

Hiroshi smiled. A patronizing smile. "Nice yak. Nice wife. Nice rice. No picture. Too far away. Even for an Instamatic, automatic, point-and-shooter. Too far away."

Then, gently, Hiroshi grasped my shoulders and turned me around to face Mount Everest. A cloud floated by the peak and the snow glistened in the early morning sun. "There is your picture," Hiroshi said. "Focus on the mountain." I found Everest in my viewfinder, standing twenty-eight thousand feet tall and slam dunking every other mountain in the neighborhood. Gently, steadily I pushed the shutter. Not a sound. Not a click. Not a picture. I was out of film. Wasted on a blue duffel, a yak, a wife, and a bowl of rice.

On the wall of my study I have hung a picture of that day at Everest. I call the photo my pointilist period. One blue dot (duffel?); one black dot (yak?); one female dot (wife?). Even though I enlarged the picture to sixteen by twenty-four inches, the rice vanished. Why would I hang this picture? A long-standing love of dots? No, the picture reminds me not to focus on the trivial; life is too brief to squander on petty concerns or events, too brief to waste looking into the valley when our vision urges us to look beyond the moment. Yes, time moves quickly, too quickly between the morning sunrise and the evening sunset.

Not long ago I received an envelope postmarked Kyoto, Japan. Inside was a picture of Mt. Everest, professionally taken with a Hasselblad. On the back of the photo I found an inscription:

> Dear Dan,
> Always remember to focus on the mountain.
> Sincerely,
> Hiroshi, your friend at 14,000 feet

On what do you focus? If you were to sit down and list a week's activity, how would the pieces of the week fall? I will give you my listing.

1. Details
2. Details
3. Details
4. Details
5. Relationships
6. Myself

When do I make the time to focus on broader interests—for instance, love, a professional dream, a hidden creative desire? I am too busy shifting my pink note slips from one side of the desk to the next. I try to write in the morning from 7:00 A.M. to 10:00 A.M. When successful I feel relaxed and content for the remainder of the day. I like to write. I feel fulfilled when I write, focused on an activity of personal worth, but Monday morning I scheduled an appointment to have my car serviced. Tuesday morning the phone rang and I spoke with my cousin. "Dan, we just returned from five days in New Orleans. Fantastic." Wednesday morning I had a 9:30 dentist's appointment. A week's writing—gone. My car does need servicing, and I enjoy talking with Cousin Roger, and the upper molar throbs; but why can't I schedule those details of my life at another time? "Discipline yourself, Dan. Discipline yourself. Why do you permit details to steal time from what you wish to focus on? Why?"

Why do I become distracted by details that:

1. Don't really have to be attended to.
2. Could be done at another time.
3. Could be done in half the time.

Beginning tomorrow I intend to set aside two hours each day for a major interest, in my case writing. Something worthwhile. I could institute that plan today but unfortunately I still have to work out the details.

PTP (Passing Through Phenomenon)

Don't Live Superficially

Woman's Times, a weekly newspaper for women in upstate New York, had grown from the basement of a suburban home into a modern brick and glass building. Shortly after the opening the publisher invited me to tour the plant. My guide, an attractive blond-haired woman in black silk pants whose youngest son Jared, "Finally went off to nursery school," led me into the newsroom where a copy editor, hidden behind a stack of Diet Coke cans, corrected an article on AIDs. From the newsroom we entered the advertising room. Ads for Sal's Pizza, Henley's Ford and The Computer Center were tacked to the cardboard wall.

It was the last room, a spartan windowless square, that sent up warning signs. First, the room overflowed with computers—my nemesis. My son Scott once speculated that if I had been born 150 years ago, the Industrial Revolution may never have occurred. He could be correct. In my youth I was allergic to dust, ragweed, cats, dogs, and chocolate. In advancing years I tested positive for technology. Entering the room where computers spewed information on circulation, advertising income, and total revenue I began to itch.

The woman operating the computer increased my discomfort. It was her cool demeanor, her slightly graying hair pulled back in a severe bun, her austere grey suit. Quietly I tiptoed across the room, hoping to escape, but she pushed "Enter" on the keyboard, fixed me with an icy stare and coolly asked, "Yes?" I froze. Swiveling in her chair she mellowed (perhaps I thawed) and we were introduced. "Ellen, this is Dan."

"Can I help you?"

"Thank you," I replied. "I don't want to disturb you. I'm only passing through."

A set of figures raced across the screen and Ellen tried to smile. Then she asked softly, "Aren't we all?"

"Excuse me?"

"You said, 'I'm only passing through.' I replied, 'Aren't we all?'"

What could I say? How do you answer the question "Aren't we all?" I did not. After staring at one another she returned to her computer.

Leaving the office I observed myself in a full length mirror attached to the door. Involuntarily I said, "I'm only passing through." My image replied, "Aren't we all? Aren't we all? Aren't we all?"

"Enough!" I shouted. "I only asked the question once!" But the echo pursued me for days. Was that how Ellen viewed her life? Passing through. From black hair to tinges of gray? Then silver? Passing from room to room, propelled by the stages of life. "Only passing through." Those words imply that we never appreciate each phase of our lives, never immerse ourselves deeply, that we neglect people and events along the way?

Since that visit to *Woman's Times*, whenever I see my reflection in a mirror I say, "I'm only passing through." And the mirror answers, "Aren't we all?"

But now I know how to answer: "I hope not. I sincerely hope not."

Welcome to the Passing Through Phenomenon; the ability to live life without knowing where you have been, what you have done, whether or not you have gained fulfillment. The test of life does not always have to register "profound" but we lose moments when we approach our years as if in a revolving door ending where we began.

You can easily identify victims of the Passing Through Phenomenon. Ask them what their week was like. Watch them open their calendars and peek at the notations. Without the calendars, they do not remember; they are in the early stages of PTP. Been there. Seen that. Done that.

In a hotel in Paris I listened to a young honeymoon couple plan their day. 9:00 the Eiffel Tower, 10:00 Rue de Rivoli, 11:00 Notre Dame, 12:00 tuna fish sandwich on a baguette, 1:00 a boat ride on the Seine. In contrast I devoted the day to sitting in the Tuilleries feeding the pigeons. Back in the hotel we compared notes. I shared my delight at watching an organ grinder with a monkey on his shoulder, taking photographs of the All France soccer team, following the progress of an artist sketching a bed of cosmos with a brightly colored red and orange ferris wheel in the background. "And how was your day?" I asked. The man flipped open his guide book and read off the day's accomplishments. "We did Rue de Rivoli. Or was it Champs-Élyseé? We did Notre Dame." Observing him turn the pages I thought, if he ever loses that book he will be lost. I don't want to do life. I want to live life. Doing is passing through. We do not receive points for the number of accomplishments in a single day.

Linger at a pond on an autumn day. When you tour a museum, headphones proclaiming, "And in Gallery 2 we see Picasso at his most mature," turn off the tape. Visit with Picasso until ready to move on. If a child asks a question, pay attention to the child and not only the questions. Don't pass through but instead let time pass by. We all have to buy groceries, pay the bills, clean the garage but if we find ourselves seduced by a moment we should stay with it.

"First I was dying to finish high school and start college. And then I was dying to finish college and start working. And then I was dying to marry and have children. And then I was dying for my children to grow old enough so I could return to work. And then I was dying to retire. And now, I am dying—and suddenly realize I forgot to live."

Are you only passing through?

The Voyage Home

Find Fulfillment Close at Hand

RALPH LEFT HOME AFTER WATCHING THE Ohio State–Michigan football game in Ann Arbor. He flew to his apartment in New York, packed two suitcases and left his family, his position as a Wall Street executive—and his life. There was no reason to leave. His alma mater, Michigan, had won but as he explained to Karen, "I'm forty-one years old and I haven't found it yet." Whatever "it" was. "I know this is fairly drastic. Perhaps I should get professional help or move all of us to our country home in Chatham. Maybe buy the general store that's up for sale; become a country squire. But I'm not ready for that. I'm going to travel."

With those words he left Karen behind, kissed Alicia and Becky, put the keys to his Bentley on the front table and called Yacht Haven in Stamford instructing them to keep his forty foot sailboat in drydock next spring. (In Ralph's defense: He waited until his children were in college. He invited Karen to join him but she did not know where Ralph was going. Neither did Ralph.) Bruce, Ralph's closest friend, argued: "You have responsibilities Ralph. To Karen. To the kids. Damn, destroy your own life if you want but what about those closest to you?" Ralph nodded in agreement then boarded United Airlines Flight 527 for Denver and his ski house in Aspen. A psychologist Karen knew suggested Ralph was on the verge of a breakdown. "Visit him. He needs you." Karen went, but unable to surmount the wall returned to New York.

Ralph kept in touch. "From Aspen I flew to Israel, worked on a kibbutz in the north, picking cotton."

"Just came back from a safari in the Sinai desert. By camel. Spent time with the monks at Mount Sinai. I even took a vow of silence. That worked for one day. You know me!"

With full beard and hair tied in a pigtail Ralph chartered a boat in the Greek Islands then "hopped over" to the Orient where he was last seen trekking out of Chiang Mai in northern Thailand.

Karen's friends were careful not to tell those jokes about finding the meaning of life in an ashram on an isolated mountain in India. Ralph was probably there!

Two years passed before Karen received her last letter from Ralph, postmarked New Zealand.

Dear Karen,

I won't be writing anymore. Next week I'm coming home, If I may still use that word. I cannot justify these years, except to say something wasn't working in New York. I had played the game for forty-one years and all I had was emptiness. Unfortunately, I still have not discovered the answer.

Why am I coming home? I suppose because I love you although you have every reason to laugh. There is a second reason. In my travels I have acquired one insight: Contentment, happiness, is not discovered out there, in distant lands—it's found within.

Where does that leave me? Us? I don't know. All I know is where not to look. In the years ahead I hope to nurture a more fulfilling home. If possible, with you.

Love Ralph

And, at forty-three, Ralph returned home, to face his most challenging journey.

Does the secret of life lie out there? At one point or another have you debated, "Should I accept what I have? Is something missing in my life? Could someone else bring me greater satisfaction?" The purpose of this book is to ask, where have I been all my life? But dissatisfaction may grow out of unreal expectations. Wisdom evolves from spending time with those closest to us in exploring how a friendship and love can be enriched, instead of expending time drifting further away from those we love. The grass may be greener on the other side of the street but it still has to be mowed! We travel the world searching for what (or whom) we believe we need and find it when we return home

In *The Little Prince*, a wonderful children's fable for adults, a little prince visits earth. The prince came from a tiny planet with three volcanoes and a rose that he believed to be unique among all the roses in the world. Touring earth he passes a garden filled with roses. Five thousand roses, each one like his own. "I thought that I was rich, with a flower that was unique in all the world; and all I had was a common rose. A common rose—that doesn't make me a very great prince."

"And he lay down in the grass and cried."

The days pass and The Little Prince meets a fox who teaches him "It is only with the heart that one can see rightly; what is essential is invisible to the eye." When the Little Prince sees with his heart he understands the roses in the garden, "Are not at all like my rose—you are beautiful but you are empty—to be sure an ordinary passerby would think that my rose looked just like you—but in herself alone she is more important than all the hundreds of you other roses—because she is my rose."

Suddenly the Little Prince yearns to return to his planet. "If you have a flower that lives on a star, it is sweet to look at the sky at night." The time has come to end his wanderings.

One of my favorite aunts was a diminutive soul named Aunt Ida. She and her toy French poodle made a yearly trip from Baltimore to New York and checked into the Plaza Hotel. Her stay in New York was marked by locating celebrities and following them on their rounds. At the end of the day she would call with a report. "Daniel, I saw Paul Newman at the corner of 57th and 5th. I followed him into Central Park. Poor Binky (her poodle) wanted to stop at a fire hydrant but I wouldn't let her. 'Binky,' I said, 'If you stop at that hydrant we'll lose Paul!' Binky understood. From the park we circled around Central Park South past the St. Moritz. For an hour I followed and then . . ." Her voice dropped. "Then I lost him." That was how her conversation always ended. "I lost him, or her." Over the years Ida lost Paul (Newman), Jackie (Onassis), Frank (Sinatra), Lyndon (Johnson), and ended the day back at the Plaza, alone with Binky. What had she achieved in her search for celebrities? Exercise? A hot dog from the Sabrett stand? A constipated toy poodle? Did she ever find what she really sought? No. Did it exist? Probably, but not on the streets of New York. Eventually Ida, like all of us, had to return home, the refrain of "I lost him" echoing in her ears. What she really lost was time, seeking a world that was not hers. The mystery of life may not lie in an ashram or on the fast paced streets of New York. It may lie at home.

We travel the earth, physically, spiritually, searching for what we believe will complete our life. We return home to find it.

Fishing Challenged

Don't Make Life a
Constant Challenge

I AM FISHING CHALLENGED.

After many years of feeding more fish than catching them, I accept the harsh diagnosis. I am fishing challenged. Fish trust me. They know I will never fasten the hook in their mouth, reel them into the boat, net them, filet them. Even though I want to. Fish trust me because they know: I am fishing challenged. I cannot catch a fish.

I am also fishing undaunted. If there is a fish in the neighborhood, and a rod, I'm out there with the best. Thus, on a hike in New Zealand, when the guide asked "Is anyone here a fisherman?" to my wife's chagrin I answered, "Yes" and volunteered to spend several hours trout fishing in a cool lake at the foot of snowcapped mountains on the Milford Track. It was the last day of the trek and we had come to a fishing shack, The Boat Shed, surrounded by meadows lush with wild flowers and a semitropical rain forest blanketed with ferns.

I knew I was in the company of serious fisherman when I saw the sign posted on the front door of the boat shed:

WANTED
WOMAN TO COOK
AND CLEAN FISH

Dig worms and
Make love
Must have good
Boat and motor
Please enclose
Picture of boat
And motor.

Evidently the feminist movement had not yet reached the south Island of New Zealand but the fish had and Graham, aware of my reputation or lack thereof, guaranteed me a fish. "Hundred percent certain." Little did he know of my ability to confound the odds.

The outlet from the river to the lake churned brown and Graham frowned. "We couldn't have worse conditions. From yesterday's rain." I did not have the heart to tell Graham the real reason for the bad condition. He had an albatross around his neck and in his boat. A fishing challenged albatross!

Eventually Graham found a place to his liking and fixed a silver lure on the end of my line. "Do you know how to cast?" he asked politely. I nodded and cast onto shore, frightening a family of ducks resting from their own fishing expeditions. Next I caught the limb of a tree, pulling off a chunk of moss. Graham, demonstrating the tact of New Zealanders, complimented me. "You have real force in that cast," and turned the boat further from shore.

After an hour without a nibble we pulled into a quiet tributary fed by an underground stream. I cast into a still pool off a sandbar. A fish jumped, silver scales reflecting in the sun. "That's where I'm going to cast," I called to Graham. "There's a fish there." Graham patted me on the shoulder: "That fish is on your line, reel him in." "What?" I replied, but in the slight chance that something had gone awry in the divine plan of who should catch and who should not catch, I reeled in a line taut with a giant trout. The fish looked at me with an expression that said: "You? I was caught by you!"

Word spread along the last seven miles of the track that I had caught a thirty-six inch trout, which at this writing has reached eight pounds and is still growing. When Marion learned of my catch she responded with the faith in her partner that accrues after twenty years of marriage. "Impossible!" Others looked at me with awe and said, "He's the one who caught the trout." I was taken off the fishing challenged list.

That night I overheard a conversation between Graham and several guides. "Yep, it was a good size fish. Still . . . you know where he caught it . . . off Massacre Point. That's where the trout line up and wait for tourists. Sure helps New Zealand tourism. Can't miss off Massacre Point."

My spirits plummeted, but after several months of consideration I have asked myself, "What's wrong with catching a fish off Massacre Point?" Easy? Okay. Why does life always have to be a challenge? Why not, occasionally, travel the more comfortable path? Find an interest, an activity that you can do without effort; restore your confidence and build upon the known.

And as a byproduct, if you catch a trout, enjoy the meal.

The Talmud asks, "Who is a happy man? He who is content with his lot." Although we aspire to grow and wish to avoid the same routine day after day there are times when we need to find a comfort level; a place and lifestyle offering safety.

One of my favorite stories of the Adirondack Mountains tells of Barton's General Store in Brant Lake. As long as there has been a Brant Lake there has been a general store near the dam where trout spill over into the river. The first store was built in 1864, but as trade boomed, in 1892 the decision was made to build a larger store. What do you do with an old general store? First, Barton moved the store onto the beach fifty yards away; then he stripped the store of the McCormack cash register and the potbellied stove where loggers sat and a fiddler played. Barton put the store up for sale but did not find a flourishing market for general stores. Finally the Palisades Hotel, a luxury resort halfway up the lake, agreed to convert the homeless store into a hotel kitchen. How do you move a store? The elders reconvened. Alvin B. offered a plan: "When the lake freezes in late December we'll hitch up a team of oxen and slide the store up the lake." And that's what they did. On a cold day, as the wind blew off Pharaoh Mountain, the store slid along the ice, passing in review before a myriad of blinking Christmas lights in lakeside cottages.

Night descends early in December. By 4:00 P.M. the sun had settled in behind Lone Pine Mountain and the oxen drivers retreated for a mug of ale. "Should be at Palisades midday tomorrow," the lead driver said. The general store, left alone for the night, rested on the ice under a half-moon. Next morning, as the mooing of cows ushered in a new day, the crew of oxen drivers returned to the lake. When the men neared the site where they had left the store, all they saw was an ice fishing shanty and a solitary fisherman. "Hey mister," they called, "See an old store around here?" The fisherman stroked his ice coated beard. "That's what happens up here in winter," he said to himself, "People go crazy." The oxen drivers felt foolish. How many people can lose a general store? Then, they noticed a periscope bobbing out of a dark hole several yards ahead. A periscope? A submarine? Not in 1892! The men went closer. A stone chimney stuck its head out of the water. "This here's our store," one of the men gasped, "Sunk on us during the night." The locals knew what had happened on that December night. Barton's General Store, resistant to change, had fallen victim to a deep depression and finally hit bottom.

Several years ago the Brant Lake Historical Committee considered placing signs at landmark sites. If the project ever gets off the ground I'd suggest one marker should be attached to a buoy on the lake, near where the store sank. The inscription?

"HERE LIES BRANT LAKE'S FIRST GENERAL STORE.

BORN 1864. DIED OF DROWNING 1892. IT DIDN'T

GO BANKRUPT. IT ONLY WENT UNDER."

At the risk of over investing a building with human qualities, I admire the general store. It knew what it was and where it belonged. If Barton's store could talk it might have said, "Leave me alone. Stop pushing." (In this case pulling.) In human terms wisdom evolves from knowing when to reach beyond our grasp and when to be satisfied. Time devoted only to the quest may be a striving after the wind.

One April 16th the son of a successful congregant sat in my study, a day after receiving his college acceptance letters from Harvard and the University of Colorado. Could there be any doubt where Alex would matriculate? His father, a Harvard graduate, had already ordered a picnic lunch for the Harvard–Yale football game; his mother had informed her bridge group and, quite mysteriously, a maroon Harvard sweatshirt appeared on Alex's bed. The only dissenter from the Harvard victory march was Alex who implored, "Rabbi, please, talk to my parents. I don't want to go to Harvard. It's too large and, anyway, I want a career in environmental science. Colorado's the perfect place but my parents think the only reason I want to attend CU is to ski. Talk to my parents. They'll listen to you."

They didn't and Alex enrolled at Harvard where he lasted through parent's weekend before dropping out. The entire family sought counseling and, one year later, Alex matriculated at Colorado. When I last heard from him he had received his doctorate in environmental studies, was employed by the state of Colorado, and lived outside Boulder. Within the family only Alex recognized where he would feel comfortable. The level may not have been what his parents wished, but content with his lot, Alex had blossomed into a happy man.

Where do you want to be on the continuum of time? Where are you comfortable? What can offer satisfaction? Those are important questions to ask if you wish to make time your own— even if you don't catch any fish.

In the Days of Rome

Build Around a Keystone

JOSEPH AND I STOOD BENEATH THE Arch of Titus. "If Titus could only see Rome now! Fiats and Ferraris," I said, thinking back to 70 C.E. when gladiators astride chariots celebrated Rome's victory over Israel. According to historians, the Roman generals Vespasian and Titus led a procession of captured slaves, followed by a golden table and lamp stand seized during the sack of Jerusalem. The record of these events was celebrated on stone reliefs of the Arch.

"Joseph, whenever I visit Rome and stand at the Arch of Titus I remember the fall of Israel, the destruction in the year 70."

Joseph smiled. "Perception, Dan, perception. You think of destruction, I think of construction. That's the difference between a historian and an architect."

"What?"

"The construction of the arch." Joseph rubbed his hand over a stubble of grey beard. "What do you know about arches?"

I shrugged.

"The arch dates to Egypt. Five thousand years ago the Egyptians used this design for underground tombs—but the Romans, they really developed the arch. Do you understand the way an arch works? Why it doesn't collapse?"

"Joseph, even if you explain I probably won't understand. I'm warning you."

Joseph didn't care.

"Good! Good! I'll explain. First, gravity. You do know about the force of gravity?"

I was still with him.

"Gravity pushes the two sides of the arch outwards. You would think the arch would collapse since the sides push away from one another. Surprising that the arch doesn't break apart once the frame is dismantled; leaving just a pile of stones. Still with me?"

I nodded.

"The secret of an arch lies in converting the thrust of the arch downward, not to either side."

My mind drifted to gladiators slaying lions outside Gucci's on the Via Veneto.

"You're losing me, Joseph."

"Hang in, Dan. One more piece, that's it. Look where the two arches meet, at top center. . . . He pointed to a block, larger than the others and tapered on either side. "That's the keystone. It buttresses all the other stones, gives them support. Inserting the keystone directs the weight downward. That's what makes the arch stand. Thank the Romans for that little invention."

Joseph and I went our separate ways, but he had given me a new appreciation of a single stone, the keystone, a necessary component in architecture and in human life.

What qualifies as your keystone?

Parents of our religious school children had gathered to discuss Christian rescuers, that handful of people who at the expense of their own lives reached out to save Jews during the Holocaust. One of the participants mused, "I don't know if I could have done that. Is there any cause worth dying for?" I thought about that question, "Is there any cause worth dying for?" and concluded the query should be phrased differently. "Is there anything worth living for?" What do you feel so deeply that it motivates your life? What is the keystone? Some might say, "My children—they are worth living for." But children grow, leave home, and then? Others may answer, "Success," but success brings only monetary satisfaction: a launching point for the next step on the rung of the ladder.

The theologian Paul Tillich taught that everyone needs an ultimate concern. When Van Gogh painted sunflowers in the fields near St. Remy he was all consumed by his passion. When Martin Luther tacked words destined to change Christianity to a church in Wittenburg he concluded, "Here I stand, I cannot do otherwise." Van Gogh and Luther stood outside of time. Consumed with inner fire, the hands of the clock did not dictate their lives.

A Hasidic Jew, a man whose life revolved around the synagogue and the Sabbath was asked, "Aren't you depressed on Sunday when the Sabbath is over?"

"Not at all," the devout man answered. "On Sunday I still bathe in the warmth of the day before."

"And, Monday? Tuesday?"

The Hasid smiled. "No, no. On those days I can think back to the Sabbath."

"Well, surely, on Wednesday you must be depressed. The Sabbath is four days past."

"Oh," the Hasid sighed, "You are correct, but on Wednesday I know the Sabbath will come again in two days and I am filled with joy."

The Orthodox Jew lived for his religion. That was his keystone. Buddha taught, "If you do not get it from yourself where will you go for it?" Most of us permit external events to shape our lives. We fill our calendars but we do not fill our spiritual needs. The keystone may change in the natural progression of the years; at one time the stone will comprise a creative talent, a loved one, work, but the test of the keystone is whether it can withstand the erosion of the years. Examine your filofax, even the scribbled notations in the margin. Are any of these the keystone to your life or only pieces destined to fall into a heap if permitted off the paper? We are an age longing for a longing; seeking a passion. If we can find this passion time will not slip from our grasp. The first step in our search is to cast away the delusion that busyness is a keystone, that time filled is the same as time fulfilled.

May your ultimate concern support your life.

PART 5

LANYARDS

On Weaving Time for Yourself and for Loved Ones

Lanyards

Weave Webs of Relationships

ON A DAY IN LATE AUGUST WHEN the red leaves of the maple tree in front of Daby's General Store foretold autumn, I bicycled around Brant Lake. I should have been home writing, but the day was too beautiful. Stopping at a friends house I watched their young daughter Katy making a lanyard. Although artistically illiterate, lanyards were the one craft I had semimastered as a child. At one time I even dreamed of someday traveling to a suk in Persia and weaving intricate carpets with Ali Baba and the other mythical characters. Instead, when the time for a career decision loomed, I decided to become a rabbi and weave words.

Sitting with Katy rekindled the spark of lanyardism and, when asked to lend my finger to hold the knot at the top of the red, white, and blue strands I responded willingly. Carefully Katy intertwined each individual strand of soft plastic until the lanyard draped over the edge of the table. I followed the result with the fascination we experience when something grows before our eyes, but too soon she ran out of threads and with a hug excused my finger. I felt sad that the project was completed. "Well, Katy," I asked, "What do you do now?" She shrugged. "Maybe I'll get more material. I'll make another lanyard." My heart raced. Would I be asked to lend another finger? Would I be reemployed instead of an out of work lanyard maker? To my disappointment Katy was not ready to make another lanyard. First she wanted to play Ping-Pong (another activity I failed as a child), ride on a jet ski (not around when I was a child), and wrestle with her brother (personally impossible since I was an only child). Would it be seemly to beg Katy to take her ball of lanyard material and begin another lanyard now? After intense deliberation I concluded this would not be appropriate behavior for a fifty-eight year old man. Instead I continued my bike trip home where I would struggle with the threads of this chapter.

While bicycling near Bent-Lee Farms, home to a herd of black angus cattle, I received an inspiration. Not an ordinary inspiration. A lanyard inspiration. Therefore I dedicate this particular chapter to Katy and her family.

The inspiration. Unlike lanyards, where there are always more strands lurking in another room, time is exhaustible. Therefore, how do we divide time in such a way that we have sufficient time for ourselves, the single strand, and for others, the woven strands? The red, white, and blue that individually and collectively bring color to our lives.

Before continuing, I share several general comments on finding time for yourself and others. First, you cannot find more time. After hours spent in Barnes & Noble scanning self-help, time management, and inspirational books, I have not discovered any books that help me find more time. (In fact, I have wasted a lot of time searching.) And if it does not exist at Barnes & Noble it does not exist. At last count the superstore shelved over five hundred books in self-help alone! Yes, there were titles telling me how to have a thirty-six hour day, but extra time does not exist. More lanyard material? Certainly. But not time.

Secondly, we do not need more time to satisfy our own strands and to weave ourselves into harmony with those we love. The time is there. We need to make value judgments. Value judgments ask us, "What is of worth?" "What are our priorities?" "Do we *want* to make more time for ourselves and for our loved ones?" If we do, we can. We will find the time *if* (a very big *if*) we wish to find the time. The secret of finding time does not reside in the sphere of time management but in the realm of desire management.

The following stories do touch briefly on how people discover the time to satisfy their own needs and the needs of others, but the more crucial discovery is the trigger that makes it worthwhile to reach out to yourself and to others. Why should you want to make time? Without the answer to that question you may say "I wish I had more time," but you will not find the time. For yourself. For loved ones.

Time management evolves from value management.

The Reverend Clergy and the Treadmill

Make Time for Yourself

"**D**AN, CAN YOU EXPLAIN WHY MY congregants bristled when I put up a 'No Trespassing sign?' They tack 'Posted' signs to the trees on their property to keep out deer hunters and solicitors, but when I post a sign the congregation rebels. And my sign didn't even say 'No Trespassing.' It was far gentler."

Reverend Claude Pike smiled. "You probably don't understand what I'm saying." I nodded in agreement.

"Well, last month I had an especially bad day. It began at 6:00 A.M. when Perry, a church elder, asked me to officiate at the funeral of the ninety-two year old mother of his sister's great aunt Matilda's friend Millie. 'I'll meet you at Millie's at 11:00 to go over details.' Then I cooked pancakes for the Rotary Club breakfast and met with a salesman from House of Lamps who demonstrated why we should use blue instead of white fluorescent bulbs in the social hall. After christening Samantha I found a homeless man in the sanctuary. He needed money for a bus to Hartford, at least that's what he said—probably for wine at Henry's Tavern. I gave him a few dollars and he blessed me on the pulpit! Said he was a deacon in his church down south. After I taught my class on "The Gospels and Global Warming" and made an appearance at the sisterhood fashion show it was still only 2 P.M."

Claude adjusted his clerical collar. "Want to hear the rest of the day? Neither did Mary when I arrived home at 10:00 P.M. She fell asleep while I repeated the invocation I gave at the dedication of the fire house. They just bought a new hook and ladder. I spoke about Jacob who saw angels climbing a ladder to heaven: 'May your new ladder lead you to the second floor where you will put out fires, save people, and so on, and so on.' Clever?"

I smiled.

"The following morning Mary apologized for sleeping while I spoke. 'Claude you need time for yourself. Time to think!' I shivered in alarm. 'Mary, you're right. I haven't even begun my Christmas sermon. This year I need a savior.' Disappearing into our son Kyle's room I seized a magic marker, tan poster paper, and drew a maze of wiggling blue lines, my portrayal of a brain. Underneath I scrawled in thick crimson letters: 'Please Do Not Disturb, Minister Is Thinking' and rushed off to tape the sign to my study door before anyone came.

"Savoring my victory I tried to think, but I was out of practice. The brain muscles atrophied from too little use. A tiny thought surfaced but the buzz on my intercom destroyed that thought. It was Mary, my secretary. "Reverend Pike, I didn't want to interrupt you by knocking but I just had to say—your sign is adorable! Simply adorable! Especially the blue squiggly wiggly's.' I heard Henrietta's voice outside the office. Usually she speaks in a whisper. Not today. 'It's a shame the Reverend's thinking' she shouted. 'I need his opinion on whether we should have tuna melt after Christmas caroling.' I tiptoed to the door and slid my reply underneath. 'No!' Later in the day the religious school teacher organized a class project, 'Letters to the Minister,' and the children left notes on the sign:

> 'Dear Reverend Pike, Do you only think religious thoughts?'
> 'Dear Reverend, when you're done thinking please return the bubble gum I stuck to the metal chair when we visited your class last week. Thank you, Chuck.'

Claude shrugged. "The next day, in the middle of a really deep thought, the president of my vestry called. 'Reverend Pike, what's this I hear about you bringing thinking into the church? Mabel telephoned to tell me it's one of those Upper West Side liberal ideas. She asked if you were really hired to think. I calmed her down, but still you might reconsider that sign. . . .'"

"So, Dan, after twenty-four hours the sign came down. I still believe I was on to something. With the pace of modern life, very few of us have time for ourselves—to think, meditate, do what we want. We even overprogram leisure hours."

Claude fixed his soft blue eyes on me. "Tell me Dan, do you think that sign was too far ahead of the times? Was I thoughtless? I need another opinion. What do you think?"

Reverend Claude Pike expressed a modest wish. Time for himself. Downtime for his own interest—in Reverend Pike's case, thinking. Who would object to granting time for oneself? Most of the immediate world! Demands invade our personal space. Be here! Do this! Until we yell out, "Help!" No one can help you find time for yourself—except yourself. Stand up. Gird your loins. Summon the courage to say, "This hour is mine. Posted. No Trespassing."

A time expert analyzed the average American's life. The extensive list included the following.

Five years waiting in line
Nine months sitting in traffic
Twenty-four years sleeping
Two years on the telephone
Eight months opening junk mail

Do we really need to spend all that time waiting in line, opening junk mail, sleeping, sitting in traffic? At the end of a week chart your allocation of time for the prior seven days. Could you make changes in the coming week that provide you with free time, new time to fashion as you desire? Probably. Use time more productively. In New York commuters actually look forward to the ride to work on erratic trains and subways. "That's when I read." "I've had a bridge game for thirty years." And if you are spared the agony of commuting, set your alarm an hour earlier. Disappear into a hidden alcove of the house, your space until the sun rises. Read, think, tinker, exercise. (But don't go on a treadmill. That's too symbolic of the remainder of your day.)

Tell yourself that you deserve your own time. You earned your own time, no matter what your age. An apocryphal story (that I hope is true) tells of Sam who received a dinner invitation. "This is Lucy. I'm having a small gathering at my home on Tuesday, January 14th. You simply must come." Sam checked his calendar. January 14th. Six weeks from now. Of course he was free. What excuse could he offer?

A pause, then his mellow voice reached Lucy. "You know how I would love to be with you and Cary," but January 14th will not be possible. That is the night I'm scheduled to dine with myself."

For those who cannot cook or are desirous of maintaining friendships I would not suggest Sam's approach, but I admire his courage. He had made a date with himself. Scheduled in time for himself. Inviolate time. Congratulations, Sam!

In contrast, when I met with Tom, a leading investor banker, before my sabbatical he expressed envy. "I've always wanted to hike in New Zealand, visit the mud people in New Guinea, rent a chateau in Provence. Always. And to travel without a set itinerary? Just go where the spirit moves you? God, Dan, I envy you."

Naively, I asked Tom why he didn't travel for six months. "Just take off. You are self-employed and financially comfortable" (an understatement).

Tom peered at me. "Dan, you don't understand. I can't leave the business."

"Even with three secretaries?"

"Even with three secretaries. Who will look after the details. Maybe after I retire. Then I'll make time for myself."

But Tom would never retire. He created busyness that took him out of himself. Retirement would be a frightening prospect for this man. In spite of his protestations, what would he do with himself? I could suggest a score of ideas, planned and unplanned for this creative man, but he would not listen. People express a desire for their own time but they fear private time. Private time forces us to confront ourselves, whether sitting in an easy chair and reading, walking on a country path, sitting on a beach. The unexamined life is not worth living—but it is safer to surround ourselves with people.

Where have I been? Where am I going? What part of my life belongs to me? No one will send you a reminder of this annual checkup, but each January 1, when you initiate a new calendar, pencil in the notation: "Yearly checkup for examination of the self. Is there any self left?"

Whose life is it anyhow?

Play Ball!

Find a Partner

"**S**ON, SHOULD WE HAVE A CATCH?"

"Sure, Dad, sure."

My father's words, barely a whisper, came from the bedroom in our house on South Main Avenue where he lay in the final stages of terminal blood cancer, but those words carried me back to a childhood ritual. It was the summer of 1945. I was eight years old.

"Play ball!" Dad and I leaned forward on the hard wooden bleachers at Hawkin's field, home of the Albany Senators. With Orrie Arnsten on the mound and Frankie Staucet, Eastern League MVP shuffling in the dirt at shortstop, the Mayor of Albany, Erastus Corning III (whose great-grandfather had been mayor in the days of President Abraham Lincoln) threw out the first ball.

I sat transfixed for nine innings and when we returned home Dad asked, "Son, should we have a catch?" Once upon a time, in the days when my father was young, he might have had a future as a ballplayer. I quote the words of my Aunt Ida who took the trolley from East Baltimore to Druid Hill Park to watch her brother Sam play sandlot ball for the Baltimore Orphan's Home: "Your father. He had that pitch, something he did with his knuckles. You should have heard everyone yelling, 'Strike 'em out Sam!

Strike 'em out!'" Then Ida would pause, let the pitch hang for a moment, before she came in with the fastball. "My Sam could have played for the Baltimore Orioles. No! I'm not kidding. That's what they said. 'Sam Wolk could have played for the Orioles.'"

Instead, my father, a rabbi, played with me in between running the bases to weddings, funerals, Sabbath services. All winter I prepared for opening day. As snow drifted against the windows I broke in my new pitchers mitt. A Rawlings. My knuckles pounded the leather until they turned brown from neat's-foot oil. At night I tied a baseball into the glove, slipped the glove under my red and black woolen blanket and fell asleep to the aroma of fresh leather. Waiting. Waiting for summer and those magical words: "Pitch it in here, son!"

When Dad played baseball he indulged in a major sacrifice. He took off his suit jacket. That was all he took off. His suit jacket. Shedding vest, gray tie, and suspenders proved too radical a concession. We took our positions, my back against the pear tree, Dad's against the apple. He chose the broader tree since I lacked control. (Soon, my dreams of being a pitcher would be shattered after walking the first ten batters I faced when P.S. 19 played arch rival P.S. 16). While he waited for my soaring curve ball I wondered if Dad ever experienced nostalgia for his days on the rubber at Druid Hill Park. Although I knew he was satisfied with his chosen profession, . . . still. And I fantasized my life as a baseball player's kid; instead of a rabbi's kid. "Play ball!" instead of "Let us pray." "You're out!" instead of "Amen." But most of all I imagined hours and hours of playing catch with my father. Traveling to fabled baseball diamonds from coast to coast.

No time to wonder. Suddenly the ball zipped out of Dad's hand in my direction. The horsehide cover flew through the air, red stitching spinning under a blue sky. Thud! Into my glove. Caught between the webbing. The ball snapped out of my hand. Back and forth. The rhythm of a baseball. Zip. Thud. Zip. Thud. And more, so much more, orbited from pear tree to apple tree. Love rode on that white sphere. Love traveling on a baseball hurtling through space, unraveling in its wake a gossamer thread bonding father and son. "Great pitch!" "Got it!" Overhead a golden ball of sunlight shone with approval.

The story is told of a child standing in a field and tossing a ball into the air, higher, higher. A neighbor passed by and asked, "Bobby, what are you doing?" Bobby answered, "Having a catch." The neighbor searched the field but all he could see was Bobby.

"Who are you having a catch with, Bobby? There's no one there."

Bobby smiled. "I'm having a catch with God. You can't see Him but I throw the ball up, way up into the air and God throws the ball back. Watch." Once more Bobby threw the ball into the air, beaming as it landed in his glove.

In summer I played catch. Not with God. With Dad. That was enough to satisfy any boy. And, years later, as I hear the echo, "Play ball," I remember my father in his vest, gray tie and suspenders; and the boy I was—in an age long since gone.

"Son, should we have a catch?"

"Sure, Dad, sure."

Words from the past but as true now as they were then. Over the years I have learned, whenever someone asks you to have a catch, treasure those words. On any playing field those words mean, "Do you want a partner?" To share love, friendship, contentment. Throwing out. Receiving. In the intricate webbing of the years there are times when we grope and other times when the person we seek is close as the apple tree covered with pink blossoms in spring; promising a rich harvest in fall.

But this is certain. Everyone needs someone with whom to have a catch, whether in times of joy or of sadness. Find that person. Treasure that person as a precious jewel. For you see, baseball cannot be played alone.

Neither can life.

I never had enough time with my father. This is evident in all of my writing. At the age of fifty-eight it stares me in the face; a brutal reminder. I never had enough time with my father. The reasons were several. First, he was devoted to his congregation; he was a pastoral rabbi who truly believed he had a calling to service the three thousand congregants of Temple Beth Emeth. Secondly, my father died when he and I were young. Dad never reached the psalmists three score years and ten. Since his death almost forty years ago there have been numerous occasions when I would have sought his wise counsel, his gentle smile—but he was gone. I never had enough time with my father.

Why did the relationship with my father work? Why, forty years after his death do I still give thanks for his presence? Because when we played catch he was there. Throwing out. Receiving. There with his heart. There with me. Totally. A partner. It was not the length of minutes spent together; it was the richness of those minutes. Would I have liked more? Of course, but time can be measured in length and in depth. My father and I drank deeply.

Today everyone speaks of family time. Skiing vacations, a week at Club Med, renting a cabin in the Adirondacks, Sunday drives. But what is the quality of that time together? Think back on where you have been. What happens when you set aside family time. Are you playing catch? Giving? Receiving?

In *Dinner at the Homesick Restaurant*, Anne Tyler wrote of a family whose gatherings always erupted into family feuds. As an antidote to his own loneliness one family member opened a restaurant for anyone homesick for a nonexistent home. The restaurant lacked partitions. The interior, from tables to kitchen, encouraged guests to come together. To celebrate the opening the owner invited his own family for dinner. By the main course they had quarreled and dispersed.

This year, just before Thanksgiving, I spoke with a matronly woman whose honesty I admire. "Gladys, what are you doing for Thanksgiving? Everyone coming home?" She laughed. "The whole brood. Kim with her New Age boyfriend from California; Sue, still looking for a man. Bruce will inform us of his financial acumen and the twins will continue their lifelong rivalry. Three days of tension, but everyone's coming. Dan, if you have the chance, stop by on Monday. I may need you!"

Hopefully your Thanksgiving was better, but if it was not then the time together was not family time. In "The Death of the Hired Hand" Robert Frost defines home as, "The place where, when you go there they have to take you." Sorry! Home is where, when you go there you feel safe, secure—a place where you are noticed. Family time is a cliché unless you can bequeath to one another the warmth lacking in the outside world. Otherwise, why waste time on those you say you love.

Every family consists of grandparents, parents, children who do want to have a catch, or at least want to give and receive. I never had sufficient time with my father. But when we played catch, we really played catch.

On Pebbles and Greetings

We Are Remembered by Small Gestures

THE BOY, DRESSED IN A YELLOW oilcloth slicker against the early morning drizzle, turned off the lawn mower and knelt in the wet grass by a tombstone. Gently he brushed the first leaves of fall off the raised gray granite footstone that read: "Samuel Wolk, D.D. March 12, 1899–May 29, 1957." Rising from the ground and leaving the imprint of his knees as a signature, he pulled the cord on the mower. Reluctantly the engine kicked over and the boy zigzagged in and out of rows of graves where broad branches of stately oaks stood guard over the generations. Standing off to one side I knew that soon the leaves would fall faster than they could be cleared and I wondered, "Do the leaves of autumn cover the ground to shield the earth from winter? To warm my father with a multicolored blanket and protect him from the northern snows?"

I also thought about the boy who cut the grass and tended my father's grave in the cemetery on Turner Road, next to the pasture where horses gamboled. Who was he? The caretaker's son? A high school student at Bethlehem Central High School? Who? And why did he stop at my father's grave? Did he know I seldom visited? Did he know my life was among the living? Or perhaps I shy away from memories that burrow into the heart, longings better left to rest on winter's barren landscape. Who was this boy? My proxy?

When he left I approached the family plot. In front of the footstone a purple September aster peeked out. A slight shiver gripped me as I stared at the rough hewn block of stone with the single word "Wolk." Along the uppermost surface pebbles had been placed, covering the entire stretch of stone.

When Jews visit the cemetery it is customary to leave small stones on the headstone as a sign of respect. Imperishable. Like memories. Who had placed them? Not me. I had not stopped by the family plot in over a year. Who had visited? Not only one person. Many. For a moment I thought back to my childhood. The house on South Main Avenue. At 6:00 P.M. my parents and I would have dinner. From 7:00 P.M. to 8:00 P.M. Dad would turn the pages of a worn black leather calendar, hesitating at a name before dialing. HE-8-3491. "Sophie, this is Rabbi Wolk. I wanted to wish you a happy birthday," and Sophie used the opportunity to unburden her heart. Once a year each member of the congregation would hear from my father. On their birthdays. At least once a year they could share joys and sadness. For an hour the calendar became my father's bible echoing the words of Genesis. "In the beginning. Congratulations."

Standing under a heavy mist of memories I acknowledged my father's life, dedicated to serving others in a congregation that grew from six hundred families to one thousand families, and as the names in the leather date book grew so did Dad's capacity to touch a community. That was what I remembered as I meditated by a headstone in the cemetery near a field outside of Albany, New York. Birth. Beginnings. I knew who placed those pebbles on the granite headstone. Sophie, Nat, Joseph. Their descendants. Members of Congregation Beth Emeth who had been inscribed in my father's calendar and engraved in his thoughts. "Happy Birthday." Those my father tended now cared for my father.

It is written in our liturgy, "We live on in the hearts and in the minds of those to whom we were precious." When we give of ourselves we are not forgotten, not even in death. So live your years that when they are no more you will be remembered, like pebbles on the gravestone of eternity.

In the distance the boy in the yellow rain slicker disappeared behind a grove of trees and the sun valiantly peered through a curtain of clouds, illuminating generations who had passed to their eternal rest.

"We live on in the hearts and in the minds of those to whom we were precious." My father was called upon for important occasions in the life of his congregation but I believe he lived on because of the little ways he touched people, symbolized by the birthday call. For many congregants this was the only contact they had with my father but they never forgot his words. "Sophie, this is Rabbi Wolk. Happy Birthday."

Finding time for those we care about does not demand many hours. A touch on a child's head while she is doing homework; a smile at your spouse when you come home, no matter how difficult the day at the office; listening to a person with empathy and understanding. Little acts of kindness. Not random. Intentional. In his autobiography, author Rupert Brooke describes the moment of departure when he sailed from England to America aboard the S.S. *Cedric*.

> I looked at the crowds that had gathered to see their loved ones board ship.
>
> Everyone seemed to have someone to hug, kiss, to say goodbye to, and I felt terribly lonely.
>
> I looked around the pier and in a corner found a young boy. Walking up to him I began a conversation.
>
> "Young man, what is your name?"
>
> "William," the youth replied.
>
> "William—that's a fine name. Well William, would you like to make a few shillings?"
>
> "Sure, of course. What do I have to do?"
>
> "When I leave," said Brooke, "and the horns echo and the smokestacks send out their puffs, I want you to wave, just wave."
>
> William was hired for six shillings and when the boat began

to move, some people smiled and some cried, some waved white handkerchiefs and some waved straw hats and I?—I had my William who waved at me with his red bandanna for six shillings and he kept me from feeling alone.

The wave of a hand, that is all it takes to cheer someone. It is easy to say, "I care about you." It takes little time. Everyone needs a wave, a smile, a reassuring gesture. In return you will be remembered and you will feel better about yourself.

Try it. It only takes a minute.

The Tombstone

Don't Bury Words

N OLD MAN WEARING A BLACK HAT AND long black suit jacket bent over tombstones scattered on the rocky incline leading up the Mount of Olives. Throughout the ages Jews had brought their beloved to this cemetery. From 1948 to 1967 the cemetery, situated in Jordan, was off-limits to Jews, but after the 1967 war the Mount of Olives reverted to Israel. Jews returned and foraged for family plots, located on the site believed to be the setting for Judgement Day. This old man in his black hat had joined the pilgrimage.

Some stones lay on their side, others were cracked, overgrown with weeds, or carted off by the Jordanians to line the path leading up to the Intercontinental Hotel. The man surveyed each stone. Who was he searching for as he worked his way up the slope? I followed him to the summit where he wiped his forehead with the sleeve of his jacket, his side curls damp against his face in the August heat. Finding a bench he collapsed in the shade of the gnarled branches of an olive tree dating to the Roman era.

"Do you mind if I join you?" I asked.

He shrugged.

"You are searching for family?"

He nodded. A lizard sunned itself on a shattered footstone encrusted with dirt. Only the letter "S" was still visible. Solomon? Sophie? Even in death peace eluded these Jews from Vilna, Kabul,

Toledo, Persia. My companion looked out across the Valley of Kidron where King David had walked, mourning the death of his son Absalom, "Absalom, Oh Absalom." The sunlight reflected off the Temple Mount, the original site of King Solomon's Temple, and the landscape shone with muted tones of beige and silver.

"Yes," he replied, "Each day I come here hoping to find my parents. Dead forty years. We sent their bodies from the old country. From Kiev. They are buried here but I can't find the stones. Gone. I come every day. Maybe I missed a stone."

"And if you find them?" I asked. "What then?"

"If. If. If I find them I will speak with them."

"Speak with them?" I asked, puzzled.

"Yes." And he hid his face behind fingers brown from the soil of the Holy Land. "If I find them I want to tell them what I should have told them when they were alive. Of my love for them. My respect for them."

His eyes clouded over. "Why did I wait until it was too late?"

Why do any of us wait to share with those we love?

The saddest words are words unspoken, conversations you meant to have and never had. Sometimes I envision the atmosphere at thirty thousand feet filled with unspoken words floating, searching for a place to land.

When would you have cheered someone close to you with the words, "I love you,"? How long would it take to say those words? When did you last call your spouse and say, "Just thinking of you"? Walk into a child's room for a quick visit before the weekly tennis game? We tend to take those we love for granted. A mother comforts her son "Dear, you know your father loves you. But, well, he keeps his feelings to himself." Unless he's at the office or playing quarterback at the Thanksgiving pick-up game in the neighbor's backyard. Why can't he express himself for the sake of his son? It only takes one minute but the response lasts for days.

On the Mount of Olives an old man dressed in black was searching for the grave of his parents and he was still in mourning. Not for their death but for the life he could have shared. And did not. Mourning for words buried under a tombstone.

Ode to Reading Wordsworth

Set Aside Sacred Time

W HAT WOULD A MAN WHO DIED MORE than two hundred years ago say about life? To explore this possibility I traveled to the town of Grasmere in the north of England and visited Dove Cottage, home of the poet laureate William Wordsworth. Taking poetic license I will postulate Wordsworth's thoughts.

Wordsworth lived in a low-slung gabled house, now a museum with guided tours. On the day of my visit rain beat on the slate roof. (Those who know the north of England report that rain always beats on the slate roofs!) Stopping briefly at a picture of Wordsworth's sister strolling in a field of daffodils I entered the poet's bedroom. The small shuttered window opened onto a garden where lush beds of daisies attested to England's wet weather. In front of the window a black leather briefcase lay on a table. "This was Wordsworth's," the guide explained. "Each year he would travel to the continent for six months with only this briefcase." Flipping open the cover the young student revealed a small opening, hardly enough space for six months on the continent. "William Wordsworth traveled with a change of underclothing, a spare shirt and his writing quill. That was all."

Sheepishly I glanced at my wife. We were also traveling for six months but when we had checked into the inn at Grasmere the porter noted that we were carrying two large duffel bags, two soft blue bags, two L.L. Bean backpacks, and "two pieces of wood" (walking sticks from India). Inside one blue bag could be found: six sets of underwear, a dozen extra shirts (T-shirts, wool shirts, cotton pullovers), a mobile drugstore, hair dryer, short wave radio, Walkman and several jars of peanut butter for emergency needs. For the sake of brevity I refrain from listing the contents of the five other bags!

I refocused on the guide who was asking: "How do you think William Wordsworth survived with so little?".

"He couldn't!" I heard my self saying, then, embarrassed, shrunk into a corner of the cottage. But he did and if I were ever to meet the ghost of William Wordsworth, as I wandered in the cavernous halls of Tintern Abbey carrying my six pieces of blue luggage, I would turn red as he displayed his own thin briefcase. Pointing to my excess luggage he might recite lines from "An Ode to Taking Refuge in Possessions."

How would I respond? (After asking Wordsworth to autograph my *Hachette Guide Book to England*.) Perhaps by citing twentieth century poetry on collecting things. Yes! I would quote the poetic slogan I saw on the rear bumper of a BMW parked in front of The Sign of the Dove restaurant; a paraphrase of the 1980s slogan: "He Who Dies with the Most Things Wins." This version read: "He Who Dies with the Most Things—Is Still Dead." Those words may not qualify as poetry comparable to Wordsworth, Shelley, Keats, but they describe a generation of gatherers filling suitcases, home, and lives with objects—not necessarily with happiness.

Patricia, a teacher at the private school where I teach, made a momentous announcement at lunch. She informed her colleagues, "We did it! We bought our fourth television set. This one's for Ryan. Now Ryan, Roger, Jason, and Lucy have their own television sets. Bingo!"

I laughed but one of the older staff, obviously out of touch with the modern world asked, "Why don't you have one set in the den for everyone to watch? Family time?"

That was a ridiculous question. One TV? When Jason wants to play Nintendo, Roger to watch the Rangers, and Lucy to imagine the day she would star on "Melrose Place"? One TV? Impossible!

Hoping to give a positive spin to the age of technology and things, I suggested, "So it's just you and Bruce in the family room. Home Alone."

Patricia laughed. "Haven't seen Bruce in four nights. He's in his study surfing the Internet."

What happened to the typical American family?

Patricia rocking in a chair before the fire, crocheting an afghan; Bruce tamping the hot coals in his pipe and helping Roger with the erector set, Lucy petting Corky the cocker spaniel, and Ryan carving a pumpkin. Family time. Ah, Wordsworth. How could you travel with one shirt and a change of underwear but without a lap top computer, a cellular phone, a pocket calculator? What did you ever do all day? Write? Speak with people? Share ideas with the London literate? Life must have been a dreadful bore.

Technology hastens seclusion and alienation. Throw a family together without a television and there is a risk of panic; until we realize the wonderful creativity and warmth that can evolve from a family embarked on a project together. Give a teenager the car, let him loose in the world of expressways, malls, and discos and bid farewell to an evening at the dining room table.

The self only exists in the context of another person; not as a spectator watching television but interacting with those close to us. That is why, after Wordsworth recites his lines from "An Ode to Taking Refuge in Possessions." I would reply with the little known poem "On the Joy of Car Pooling." I believe in car pools (limited to four a day). Car pools permit the rare opportunity of sharing time together, talking, listening to children's needs' unless Bobby is hidden behind the bag of groceries and Rover the Irish setter sits on little Cara.

Traditionally the Sabbath mandated time for family to be together. In Judaism from sundown on Friday to sundown on

Saturday the family shared time; work, travel, and even TV, yes even TV, were forbidden on the Sabbath. God knew what He was doing when God instituted the Sabbath. A smart move. Forget the religion's rituals—that's a matter of choice—but spend the time together as a family. Sacred time. Some families still set aside sacred time; an hour, an evening, a day when family comes together. For sacred time to succeed, the same hours should be set aside each week. Without this structure they will never happen.

A congregant's son, Ben, visited me before his freshman year at Princeton. In four years of high school he had amassed an impressive record: valedictorian, captain of the football team, homecoming king. I congratulated this attractive young man. "Ben, you really have it all. Good luck."

He smiled. "Not quite all, Rabbi."

"What's missing?"

"I would have liked more of my parents. They're great and they've given everything to my sister and me. A terrific house. A car. Camp. Trips to Europe in the summer. Aspen in the winter. But it's funny, Rabbi, I would have liked a little more of them."

We would all like a little more of those close to us; our spouses, our children, our parents, our friends. Instead of concentrating on what we have, concentrate on who we have.

And read Wordsworth.

The Trail Marker

Do Not Be a Single Heart

I N FRANCE, HIKING TRAILS ARE MARKED BY symbols on wooden placards. A single carved heart signifies the easiest trail; two hearts a slightly more difficult route. The most difficult trails are marked by the image of four hikers. Très difficile.

On a warm summer's day Marion and I shopped in the market of Bedoin, a quaint village nestled at the foot of Mount Ventoux, Provence. Filling our back packs with picnic foods we decided to follow a two heart trail. The markers led past a stucco house guarded by a German shepherd, the Bedoin Tourist Agency and soon disappeared into a meadow highlighted by the last of the spring poppies. The trail was clearly marked and at every turn, before Marion and I could ask, "Where should we go?" we spied the two hearts nailed to a tree. After wandering past a campsite with the sign "Camping au Naturel" (a nudist camp), we circled an abandoned quarry and made our way into a vineyard where we rested, waving to a passing cyclist dressed in yellow and blue colored spandex shorts. After a meal of chicken, bread, and wine we set off on the second half of our eight kilometer hike, refreshed and confident that the ever present two hearts would lead back to Bedoin and a Perrier with lemon on the Rue Cours.

The following week I returned to Bedoin to work on a

photographic essay of the markets of Provence. These century-old village markets display their goods in a manner enticing even the devout nonshopper. A display of vervein soap in a muted green tone, miel (dark beige), lavender, violet, cream colored almond and, to keep you on your toes, brown bars of vanilla soap, almost force you to be clean! At the very least to buy enough bars to assure overweight baggage on the flight home. The olive vendor exhibits twenty-seven varieties of plump olives; jars of lavender, tillul, and rosemary honey covered by gold tops decorated with bee hives catch the sun light and cherries spill off stands.

The market ended promptly at 12:00. The last wispy strands of pink cotton candy floated over a table bursting with goat cheese. A blond haired girl wearing a pink T-shirt and skin tight black shorts with slits in the side loaded cartons of honey nougat into a van departing for Avignon. Bedoin returned to its sleepy small town flavor. Reluctant to leave the calm of Bedoin, I planned another hike in the countryside. Since Marion had remained at the chateau where we were staying I chose the shortest and easiest walk. One heart. Six kilometers, one and a half hours. But this time I could not find the trail. I wasted the first forty-five minutes of the hike searching for a trail marker. I passed the shuttered vegetable stand five times, the road sign to Avignon three times and the closed tourist office four times. The second forty-five minutes I drank Anise Syrop and water at a cafe next door to the Hôtel de Ville. In brief, I never took the hike. Driving back to Chateau Unang where I was staying I pondered the metaphysical question: How can a path marked "Easiest," be so difficult to find? Next time I returned to Bedoin I would bring Marion, then we could find our way.

Why did I lose my way? Genealogists of Wolk family history suggest, "Dan you are descended from a long line of people lacking a sense of direction. Live with it." A Bedoin resident claimed that the one heart trail markers rotted out the previous year. "Bad wood." But I have a different theory. Single hearts that travel alone lose their way in life; whether in the south of France or closer to home. The old-time resident of Bedoin, informing me that the one heart wooden markers had rotted, may have been correct. A single heart withers.

How can you make time for others? By acting on the wise counsel of Lord Chesterton. "The best way to love someone is to realize you may lose them." When you realize you may be a single heart you find the time.

Recently I made two pastoral calls to the hospital. The first visit was to a young woman who had undergone a successful operation for breast cancer. She would be fine; there were few words I could say. Instead I listened; not to the woman but to her husband, a man visibly shocked by the trauma of discovering what we all know but don't want to admit—that we are vulnerable. "What would happen if I lost Susan? I always assumed she would be here forever. And now?"

He ran his hand through red hair beginning to thin. I waited.

"Dan, I don't think my life will ever be the same. Although I have always loved Susan, that love is burnished now with a brighter glow, a desire to spend more time together, to be there for her."

The second visit was occasioned by a phone call. "Rabbi, Betsy gave birth this morning. In Northern Westchester Hospital. Three months early. She was due in April. Would you stop by?"

Betsy lay in a bed, attempting to unravel her immediate future. "I'm not pregnant. I'm going home from the hospital. And I don't have a baby. Carl and I had just begun Lamaze classes; we were going to be like every one of our friends. We aren't."

Betsy's husband sighed. "I just want to hug my baby and know he will be alright."

The doctors had assured Betsy and Carl that their two pound baby would be fine, but husband and wife had ventured onto the edge of life. The baby became even more precious. While they spoke I remembered a similar premature birth. The parents had delayed naming the child until at four and a half pounds the baby left the hospital. Then the parents named their child Zechariah. "God remembers." And so did the parents.

Frances Gunther was not as fortunate as the couples I

visited and, in the last chapter of *Death Be Not Proud* by John Gunther, she wrote:

> All the wonderful things in life are so simple that one is not aware of their wonder until they are beyond touch. Never have I felt the wonder and beauty and joy of life so keenly as now in my grief that Johnny is not here to enjoy them. Today, when I see parents impatient or tired or bored with their children, I wish I could say to them, "but they are alive, think of the wonder of that! They may be a care and burden, but think, they are alive! You can touch them—what a miracle!"

Ask yourself, "How would I feel if someone I loved were not here? If one of the hearts was removed from my life's path." Ask and then act in response to your answer. Hours will free themselves in a previously impossible schedule.

The best way to love someone is to realize you may lose them. May you remind yourself before you become a single heart.

Tending Sunflowers

Plant and Live in Pairs

RESTING AT A MILE POST ON THE Grand Randonee, the hiking trail cutting across France, I leaned against a stone bridge stretching over a stream. In a windblown field a single spindly sunflower, buffeted by the weather, wobbled on its stalk. How had this lone sunflower lost its way, taking root in a field of wheat? Had the seed been carried by a sudden gust of wind when a farmer plowed his field of sunflowers? The golden flower, abandoned to its solitary fate, struggled by the side of the road.

Contemplating this stray flower I heard the barking of a dappled brown and white dog. He seemed a friendly sort and I held out my hand in greeting. Sniffing the proffered hand the dog decided (in the interest of French–American relations) to befriend me. Introductions behind us, we rested on the edge of the bridge enjoying early morning sunlight. The dog, bored with the lack of action, started off along a path cutting through the wheat field. She would run a few feet, return and lick my leg, then start off again. After three or four licking episodes I understood the dog wanted me to follow.

At the far end of the field I heard a faint cry, "Daisy! Daisy!" in the local French dialect. The dog's ears perked up and she raced toward a rusty white Renault with mud caked wheels parked on a dirt road at the edge of a broad expanse of full, glowing sunflowers. Tail wagging, Daisy nuzzled up to an elderly couple sitting on the car's running board and drinking coffee. A man in dark overalls rose and moved slowly in my direction. "Bonjour," he greeted, extending a leathery hand marked by brown aging spots. His wife, wearing baggy brown pants and a torn straw hat, offered words of welcome but since I did not speak French we communicated by smiles and "Bonjour, Bonjour,"

During my stay in France I often visited that elderly couple who moved slowly through the field of sunflowers, weeding, tilling the soil, and harvesting the flowers. Daisy would greet me with a wag of her tail (we were beyond barking) and the dog's owners shared their cheese and wine with me.

I admired those farmers who had planted many seasons of sunflowers together. They seldom spoke but, with a quiet understanding nurtured over time, they lived in harmony.

I think of the French couple walking through rows of sunflowers and contrast their presence and the dance of the sunflowers with the solitary flower near the bridge where I met Daisy. When the season ended that lone sunflower would have scattered its own seeds. I hope they grew in pairs. We do not grow well alone. Even under the warm sun of Provence.

At a sensitivity workshop in New York the facilitator instructed:

> "Complete this statement. 'I am a pen.'"
> A tall red headed man replied, "I am a pen, I write with red ink."
> A middle aged woman, "I am a pen, don't smudge me."
> A thirty something, "I am a pen, where is my pencil?"

A pen and pencil. A set. Few people want to be alone, but so many are alone, severed by divorce, unable to commit.

Perhaps one reason for the large percentage of singles is the unwillingness of couples to devote the time to make a relationship work.

When I sit with couples for premarital counseling I ask, "Why do you want to marry one another?" Assuming the couple does not flee after this question they usually answer "I love him." "She's my best friend," but I never let them off that easily!
"And?"
"And?"
"And?"
Exhausting the "ands" I listen as Becky and Rob explain that they want to be married because they enjoy being with one another; they love to do the same things; they focus on the other's needs. And they do. At the moment. But what happens after marriage? Often one or both believe the work is behind them. They forget that marriage is only an opportunity for happiness, not a gift. They have to continue working in the field of love. Spend time together. Worthwhile time. Sharing after marriage as they shared before. But children intervene, business ambitions take over, and gradually the couple take one another for granted and drift into their own interests.

A mother asks, "Do you think our children will have a good marriage? Are they right for one another?" Fifty percent of marriages end in divorce and I would propose (excuse the double entendre) seventy percent of the fifty percent who divorce are right for one another; or could be right for one another if they chose to take the time to work on their marriage.

One of the more enigmatic verses in the book of Genesis tells of the marriage of Isaac and Rebecca. "And Isaac married Rebecca and he loved her." When I teach Bible at the neighboring School of the Holy Child an astute student always says, "Rabbi, the order is wrong. The Bible should read, 'Isaac loved Rebecca and he married her.'" Yes. In the twentieth century. But maybe the biblical writers were wiser. Love, a deep love, grows out of marriage. It grows slowly, with effort, with time devoted to your partner. The biblical approach may be more effective than the contemporary statement: "And Isaac loved Rebecca, and he married her, and he divorced her." Of course, in the best of all possible worlds, the phrase would read, "Isaac loved Rebecca, and he married her, and he put aside an hour each day, or a day each week to nurture that love and love her more." That is a convoluted sentence but I hope accurate.

On the Friday of Robin's birthday Bob called his wife. "I'll be home at 5:00. Pack for the weekend. Casual." Puzzled, Robin waited for Bob who hustled her into the car and drove to a secluded inn on the New York–Connecticut border. A fire glowed in the living room of the nineteenth century converted farmhouse and the first snowfall of winter blanketed the adjoining red barn with a soft white cover. "Happy Birthday, Hon. We'll be alone until Sunday." Television ads portray that special moment, a birthday, an anniversary when the husband presents a diamond ring to his wife who gasps, flings her arms around the man and cries, 'Oh Darling! Darling! Darling!" Why don't television advertisers feature a weekend in the country, a picnic on a beach, a horse and carriage ride through Central Park? The gift of time spent with a loved one is priceless. Those two hours spent together rejuvenate those who care about one another. "When you care enough to give the very best"—give time.

We create walls of indifference erected by layers of time not well spent together. In this era of space we send a station into orbit to circle for eternity. Once in orbit we have accomplished our task. Marriage cannot be sent into orbit to circle without effort (although we may experience occasional highs). Love is often a prosaic ebbing and flowing, not always in rhythm. When our lives are at an ebb we need to increase the time spent with those about whom we care.

In today's complicated society professionals are offered refresher courses. A two-week computer course. A real estate course. A medical seminar. Only marriage seems exempt from refresher courses. Margaret Mead proposed three marriages in every lifetime. First, a romantic marriage; find that partner who sets you on fire. Second, find someone to share parenting. Third, choose a partner for the companionship of old age. Although Mead's proposal would benefit the caterers there should be an easier way to accommodate growth. Take the time to work with your partner. "But I can't find the time!" More time is spent finding a new love than finding love with one you already know. Spend the time. It could be a valuable investment.

Why? Because it is more pleasant to plant in pairs.

Why? Because every pen seeks a pencil.

Paris Time–Tokyo Time

Sacrifice for Those You Love

GENEVIEVE AND I SAT IN THE COURTYARD of an outdoor cafe when the roar of a motorcycle gang, led by a cyclist dressed in blue pants and a yellow shirt and blowing a French horn, jarred the silence of the Provencal town. Women in housedresses watering their geraniums stared in disbelief; an old German shepherd lifted his head, the first movement out of that dog since we had arrived; the waitress fled for cover behind the doors of the Hôtel de Liberté. Too late. The cyclists surrounded the waitress at the entrance and serenaded her with a French chanson.

Genevieve, a curator at the Louvre, who had come on vacation to the village of Sault sighed, "Ah, Monsieur, for this I did not need to leave Paris. Perhaps we should go?" "L'Addition," I called to the waitress who had joined the cyclists in singing "Pour Un Flirt." Turning to Genevieve I asked, "What time is it?" Genevieve took off the eyeglasses she had stored in the crest of her long blond hair, unbuttoned the sleeve of a beige silk shirt and examined a gold watch bordered with cut diamonds.

"Monsieur Daniel, do you wish to know the time in France?" Whimsy played around her mouth as I considered her question.

"France? What other options do I have?"

Nonplussed Genevieve replied. "Tokyo. It is 4:00 P.M. today in France, 6:00 A.M. tomorrow in Tokyo. Do you have a preference? French time? Japanese time?"

I looked at her suntanned wrist, the first brown spots of age concealed under the shirt sleeve. The casing of her watch enclosed two separate faces, one marked "France," in tiny letters, the other marked "Japan."

Genevieve was silent. I mused. "A watch with two time zones. Why? When you feel too far ahead of yourself you look at French time? When you want extra hours you go by Japanese time? Oui? Or perhaps this is the newest Parisian style. Next year everyone in New York will be on East Coast time, and New Guinea time, or Indiana time and Indonesia time." Genevieve replied, "No Monsieur, no."

"Ah ha! Let me guess again. Maybe you are a two-timer! Do you know what that expression means?"

"Oui, Monsieur Daniel. Oui." Genevieve laughed. "And I like your explanation. Very good. My friends in Paris are much more prosaic. They think I'm eccentric, 'Comes from spending too much time in museums,' they say. But no, no, there is a practical reason I live my life on Paris time and Tokyo time."

I counted out thirty francs for the bill, received a smile from the waitress who rejoined the motorcycle club and listened to Genevieve's explanation.

"I write books on art. My publisher and editor are Japanese. They do marvelous work in Japan, especially on illustrated plates. Akira and I often speak but I never remember the time in Tokyo. I'm on my exercycle in the morning and Akira is asleep after a long night. Last year, after too many abortive phone calls, Akira gave me this Rolex watch for my birthday, which I should mention occurs fourteen hours later in Japan! Now we are on the same time. At least we know each other's time. When one is asleep and one is awake how can you communicate?"

As if impressed by this reasoning the French horn blew a mighty blast.

Akira and Genevieve synchronized time but in real life they were not in sync. Akira was still asleep when Genevieve was on the exercycle. They were not really together. Sometimes we have to be in the same place as those closest to us, not only on the face of a watch but also geographically. And sometimes we do not want to be where family or friends desire.

For instance, Jim and Terri gave birth to a hockey son. Ice drew Jared to its glistening surface at an early age. Family records suggest Jared skated before he walked. Jim and Terri believed in furthering their son's interests. Every Saturday morning at 4:00 A.M. they grabbed a bagel and drove their son to the Tarrytown rink. The remainder of the day the rink was booked. Years passed. Jared excelled. His parents awoke earlier and earlier. Slowly they acquired an aversion to ice, any kind of ice. Jim drank his scotch straight up instead of on the rocks. Terri gave up ice cream, even Ben and Jerry's Heath Bar Crunch. Ice! Bah humbug! But the loving couple hid their feelings about ice from Jared. History would praise them for putting their feelings on ice.

Why did Terri and Jim continue to drive Jared to the ice skating rink? Why did Terri and Jim drive on wintry roads to watch Jared play left wing on the Middlebury hockey team? Why? Because Jared loved hockey and Terri and Jim loved Jared and sometimes you have to make time for your loved one's interests, even when they are not your own.

More than synchronizing watches we need to synchronize lives. Any soccer mom can tell you that! So can Terri and Jim.

A second example. David and Laura met with me before their wedding. I asked what marriage meant to them.

David: "It means going to the Impressionist exhibit with Laura. I hate art."

Laura: "It means sitting with David on a rainy, cold Sunday afternoon at the Meadowlands and watching the Giants lose. I hate football."

Sensitive to a potential danger I praised David and Laura. "I admire your desire to spend time with your partner."

Then I offered the gift of forgiveness. "David, you don't have to see every Impressionist painting. Forget Pissaro's early period."

"Laura, when the Giants play Dallas stay home."

Only Solomon, who suggested cutting a baby in half had

offered deeper wisdom. Laura and David still credit me with assisting in the success of their marriage. Willingly I accept the credit!

To find time for your loved ones implies finding time for what they want to do, even if their interests are not your own. Over the years husband and wife, parents and children move in different directions. Yogi Berra said, "When I came to a fork in the road I took it." We are always coming to a fork in the road; one the fork we would choose, the other the fork a family member would choose. Unlike Yogi Berra we cannot take all the forks. This was the dilemma faced by the recent Secretary of Labor Robert Reich who wrote an article in the *New York Times*, "My Family Leave Act," on why he was quitting a job he loved. "For several years now, I've been trying to find a better balance between work and family, and failing miserably. I've only just understood why. It's the word "balance" that threw me. I've always assumed that a better balance meant more of what you really want to do and less of what you don't. For me, and perhaps many others, that's just not possible.

"Sure, I've met lots of people who have found a better balance through doing less work and gaining more family. That may be hard to achieve economically, but for some it's at least possible. Live cheaper, scale back, give up the rat race.

"I've even met a few people who've done the reverse. For them, a better balance means more work and less family . . . .

"I know someone who found balance by cutting back on both . . . .

"But what if you're like me and, I suspect, many others? You love your job and you love your family, and you desperately want more of both. You're doubly blessed, in a way—but here's the rub: There's no way of getting work and family into better balance. You're inevitably short changing one or the other, or both."

One night Reich called home to say good night to his boys. One son asked his father to wake him up when he came in, no matter how late. "I just want to know you're here with us." That conversation convinced Reich there was not a better balance. "I've been kidding myself into thinking there is one. The metaphor doesn't fit. I had to choose."

Reich resigned his position as Secretary of Labor.

There comes a time when, like Reich, we have to prioritize and make a decision. Reich will find another position, one that will use his expertise and also permit him to resolve his dilemma in the way he chooses. Rank your own priorities. Can you balance them? If the answer is "No," Robert Reich's struggle deserves serious consideration.

Working families also feel the pressure of making choices. If both partners work family time may suffer. Faced with this dilemma certain families decide to scale down their lifestyles freeing one parent to work part time or not at all. If this is impossible then time spent with children, especially weekend time, should be of the highest quality. One father told me, "My wife and I, we're touching too many bases—and I'm not sure we're doing anything well." Time to cut back, examine priorities, accept compromises. Income might decline; you will not be a partner or CEO this year—but what have you gained? Only you can answer. The best of all possible worlds does not always permit us all possible worlds.

No matter how we set our watches, when one person is in Tokyo and the second person is in Paris, life is not synchronized.

The Man in the Box

Take the Time to Empathize with Others

H E INTRODUCED HIMSELF AS The Man in the Box, a well-dressed man in a three-piece black suit, a white and gray polka dot tie, and polished black shoes. We were riding on the 5:30 Metro North train from Grand Central to Mount Kisco and shaking his hand I searched for an impressive title like "Man in the Box"—all I could think of was, "My name's Dan."

My companion laughed. "Actually I'm Ryan and I live off Route 128 near the Armonk border."

I nodded. "Near Ben and Jerry's?"

"Right."

I put aside the *New York Times* and asked, "Why do you call yourself 'The Man in the Box?'"

"I hoped you'd ask," he smiled, obviously pleased with himself.

"This morning I had a business meeting on the Upper West Side. I'm an accountant and this was a long-time client. There was a cloudburst on 89th Street and I searched for cover under an awning but couldn't find any. Next to a fire hydrant I saw one of those huge packing cartons lying on its side. Once held a GE refrigerator. I dashed for the box and crawled inside. Sound strange?"

I shrugged.

"Well it does to me," he continued. "Just an impulse. But that's why I have to tell the story. The carton worked. I stayed dry and soon the rain stopped. I began to ease my way out of the box but in a far corner I saw a dirty red sleeping bag. A few shirts, ripped at the elbows, lay on top the sleeping bag and an empty bottle of cheap wine. This was someone's house!"

Ryan, alias "The Man in the Box," crossed his legs. "I abandoned the carton, hoping no one had seen me, took one last look and hurried on to my appointment. All day I've wondered who lived inside that GE carton. Was it one of those homeless men who beg for money at the 96th Street exit ramp of the West Side Highway? How long had he lived there? What will he do in winter? I don't have any of the answers but I'm sure glad I'm not him. Can you imagine living in a GE carton?"

The train pulled into Mount Kisco and we went our separate ways, but driving home I repeated Ryan's questions: "Who lived inside that GE carton?" "Was it a homeless man?" "How long had he lived there?" "What will he do in winter?"

I imagined Ryan sharing his unusual sojourn with his wife over a glass of white wine and I wondered if the experience might have any lasting effects on this suburban commuter. For instance, after ten minutes in a box would Ryan better understand those who are helpless?

The homeless man who lived in that box represented anyone who, at one time or another, feels adrift and seeks protection from the storms of loneliness, sadness, disappointments. That may be anyone of us. We can live in luxury homes and still feel abandoned. If you have ever experienced the fear of isolation, is it possible that you will find the time for others?

One hundred and fifty years ago Henry David Thoreau wrote: "America is a place where millions of people are lonesome together." Have you ever felt lonely? Bereft? Did someone come along at that moment and, by offering several moments of their time, lift your spirits? If so, you will find time. When was the last time you were asked to reach out and said, "I'm too busy." Were you?

On occasion we all feel invisible . . . no matter what our age.

Said the little boy "Sometimes I drop my spoon."
Said the little old man, "I do that too."
The little boy whispered, "I wet my pants."
"I do that too," laughed the little old man.
Said the little boy, "I often cry."
The old man nodded. "So do I."
"But worst of all," said the boy, "it seems
Grown ups don't pay attention to me."
And he felt the warmth of a wrinkled old hand.
"I know what you mean," said the little old man.

(from "The Little Boy and the Old Man,"
SHEL SILVERSTEIN)

Time spent only on the I can be very lonely. When Jews sit down at the Passover Seder to recount the story of the Exodus in Egypt they are reminded to "remember the stranger in your midst, for you were strangers in the land of Egypt." Devoting two hours once a week, once a month to the community will ease the pain of the stranger and humanize the world.

Why give to others? Why make the time in your already overprogrammed schedule to work at a soup kitchen, a temple or church homeless shelter, to be a support person for an immigrant newly arrived in this country? (Perhaps following the same dream as your parent or grandparent.) Why? Because today it is another; tomorrow it may be you.

Martin Buber classified relationships as I–It and I–thou. An I–It relationship treats the person as an object; the I–thou as someone created in the image of God—special, unique. *Human.* At one time or another all of us feel like objects. For instance, not long ago my phone rang and I heard that annoying voice on the other end.

"Hello. This brief message may change your life!"

I remember thinking, No! No! No! Another computer message on 967-8745, my unlisted phone number. Only computers know unlisted numbers. What was the robotic voice plugging today? "Pink Sludge Herbal Tonic?" "Fifty ways to rent a vacation home in the Bosnian countryside?" "A trial offer to the best-selling book *Great Computers I Have Known.*" Why? Why do I listen to computer messages? I always succumb. That's the way I am. "If you wish to use our automatic system please punch in your thirty-seven digit credit card number, your Social Security number, date of birth, and the last fifteen lottery numbers you played. Followed by the pound sign."

Somedays I never experience human contact. I simply let my fingers do the walking on my push button phone. However, one memorable day, I dialed Metro-North for the train schedule between Mount Kisco and Grand Central Station. A strange sound drifted out of the phone. For several moments I failed to distinguish the noise but gradually a memory of bygone days surfaced. This was a voice. A real human voice. Like the kind I remember from PC days (pre-computer days). The voice said: "Can I help you sir?" Shocked, I forgot my question. Instead I stammered:

"Good morning."

To my amazement, the voice replied "Good Morning."

What could I say next? How could I adjust? Collecting myself I explained, "I didn't expect a real human voice."

The woman's voice at the other end of the phone sounded embarrassed. "I'm sorry, sir. On behalf of the company I would like to apologize. Our computer is down. Instead you have to speak to me. We are sorry for the inconvenience. Hopefully I can help. If not, the computer message should return in an hour. Please call back."

Help? She had made my day. Every fifteen minutes I called this train dispatcher. Delighted in a real human voice. I called all day. Ah, Brave New World! You arrived. Unfortunately, at 4:00 P.M. they fixed the computer and the staccato voice reappeared. "Push the first ten letters of your destination. . . ."

Usually I am okay with computer messages (not really!) but some days I want that real voice; I am the Man in the Box. When have you felt like an object? Whenever I pay the toll at the Henry Hudson Crossing, buy a subway token, hold for a doctor, narrowly avoid a collision with a child on a skate board I feel like an object. That is when I promise to be attentive to others. I'm not always successful but I try. And then I think of myself living in a cardboard carton.

Any I try a little harder

Amen! Amen!

Everyone Needs a Backup

L
OUISE LIVED BY THE MOTTO: "You just got to keep on keepin'
on." At the age of ninety she still traveled from Albany,
New York to St. Louis, Missouri to march with her AME
Zion Baptist Church. And at ninety, although she no longer made
matzo balls for our seder—"The kind that feel just right . . .
they don't crumble and they don't need a steak knife to cut,"—
Louise still cleaned my mother's apartment every Monday and
Thursday.

"How do you find the energy to work at ninety?" I asked.

Her face a patchwork quilt of years, Louise answered, "Well,
Daniel, I guess I just keep on keepin' on."

Those words were only a kernel of the wisdom I gleaned
from Louise. When I was twenty-one, after returning from a year
in Israel, she had asked me to deliver the Sunday sermon at her
white clapboard church on the north side of Albany. "Tell about
your year at the University." Dutifully I gave a talk on the Hebrew
University, my academic studies, student life—and, in the record
time of five minutes, I anesthetized an entire congregation.
(This time, incidentally, still stands as my personal best although
several sermons came close to breaking the mark.) At the end of
page two I mentioned that the Hebrew University stood atop a
biblical hilltop in the city of Jerusalem. Suddenly my congregation

of black worshippers erupted. "Jerusalem! Amen! Amen!" Realizing I was on to a hot word I began the next sentence, "In Jerusalem . . ." and there they were again, responding, "Amen! Amen!" Who said it was difficult to be a hell fire and brimstone preacher? You only need the key words. Gaining confidence I laced my next sentence with "Jerusalem," "Israel," "Holy Land." Hands waving in every direction, one hundred black men, women, and I soared into the rafters.

Following services Louise hugged me to her ample bosom. "You were mighty grand, Daniel. Mighty."

Pleased with my first experience as an old time preacher I replied modestly.

"A little rocky at first Louise. Thought I lost them."

"You caught on fast, though. Real fast. Once you said 'Jerusalem' you spoke to their hearts, Daniel. Yes sir. 'Jerusalem,' 'Holy Land,' that spoke to the heart. Seems to me Daniel, good preachers, they speak to the heart, not the mind. Matter of fact, seems to me everyone who really wants to reach someone else should speak to the heart."

At the age of ninety Louise spoke to the heart, a heart that beat rapidly as she climbed the steep steps to my mother's apartment on South Allen Street. Resting against the wall to catch her breath Louise waited for my mother, a spry eighty-five, to open the door. Recently my mother had pleaded with Louise. "You're too tired to clean. And the trip from Northern Boulevard. The bus. The walk in snow from New Scotland Avenue. Louise, come to visit. Join me for tea, not to clean."

Louise, faithful to her belief, "You just got to keep on keepin' on," would have nothing of my mother's suggestion. "Been with you for thirty-five years, Missus Wolk. Not going to stop now. Don't work as fast as I once did. No Ma'am," and she threw in another Louise-ism, "'But bit by bit the basket gets full.' That's what my grandpappy would say when he was out in the fields picking cotton. 'Bit by bit my work gets done,'" and Louise would trudge about the apartment, unable to see the cobweb intricately stretched over the windowsill. Most Mondays she knocked over the African violet, muttering softly, "Needs a bigger table. Shouldn't be here, this African violet." A year earlier my mother had declared the Harvard Wedgwood plates off limits to Louise after she dropped a blue and white ceramic Delft vase from Holland.

About 1:00 Louise would pass judgment, "Real clean, Missus Wolk. Way a house should be." With a sigh, she would start down the stairs, calling after her, "I'll be back on Thursday. Hear?" My mother would also sigh, take the broom, sweep up the dirt from the African violet, repot the traumatized plant, dislodge the spider from the web and dust the dishes. Finishing her work at 4:00 P.M. mother would settle into the couch and pass judgment. "Real good, Louise. The way a house should be."

The day came when my mother could not clean up the African violet, who then decided enough was enough and died. The dishes had acquired a thick film and the spider had invited family from all over Albany to spin a web any spider would be proud of. That was when we hired Rhonda, who worked at the Fisher's, mother's next door neighbors.

Visitors to the South Allen Street apartment on Monday and Thursday witnessed the following domestic scenario. At 10:00 A.M. Louise struggled into the apartment and after a cup of strong English Breakfast tea made her rounds with broom and dustpan. At 1:00 P.M. my mother made futile attempts at cleaning up after Louise. Finally, at 4:00 P.M. Rhonda cleaned the house. Frustrated by ownership of a cleaning company, I considered retiring my mother and Louise, perhaps giving them a testimonial dinner and presenting each woman with an African violet and a gold pin in the shape of a spider. But, as the weeks passed, I mellowed. Who is self-sufficient? Who can tie up all the pieces of their life alone? Everyone needs someone as a backup. How could I retire Louise and my mother? Whatever they did, or did not do, they acted out of love. Louise for my mother, my mother for Louise and both women for the home they had, in so many ways, shared for almost half a century.

These two white haired women, soon to enter a home far

removed from South Allen Street, acted from the heart. All I could say was:

"Amen! Amen!"

Rhonda, my mother, and Louise were independent women, nobly struggling with vicissitudes that entered their lives. But independence is illusory; we all need someone to pick up after us— whether or not we own an African violet or a spider web. When we find the time to be there for someone in need, he or she will reciprocate.

Once, trekking in Nepal I arrived at a suspension bridge. The group I was with recoiled at the sight of the swinging bridge but, determined to demonstrate our rugged posture we refused to show fear. Marion, true to form ("If they build it I will jog"), jogged across. I walked slowly, pausing in the middle to photograph the fast flowing waters below. (When developed the fuzzy pictures testified to a quavering photographer.) Sven, a macho experienced hiker fell on all fours and crawled. Only Britta expressed the need we all felt. Calling out to a Sherpa guide she closed her eyes, took his hand and crossed. It only took a minute for that Sherpa to lead Britta to the other side but I was certain some day Britta would take a moment to support someone else crossing a precarious point in their lives.

Families in mourning pride themselves on showing strength. "Joan is strong. Not a tear. She'll be okay." Will she? Strength lies in admitting our needs, our desire for backup. The alternative is a life cluttered with spider webs, spilled African violets and a gauntlet of obstacles.

Are you independent? How independent? Have you ever cried out for help? Was someone there? A Louise? A Rhonda? A parent? A friend? Will you be there for them?

Take the time.

PART 6

YOU ONLY
LIVE TWICE

Making the Most of Time

YOU ONLY LIVE TWICE

Making the Most of Time

L IKE THE HANDS OF A CLOCK, THIS BOOK HAS COME full circle and now, at the end (or is it actually the beginning?) I will explain the inspiration for writing *The Time is Now*. The book evolved out of a dream.

In the dream a member of my congregation followed me onto the pulpit and handed me a box wrapped in blue paper. A muffled sound escaped. "Tick. Tick. Tick." A bomb? "Tick. Tick. Tick." Cautiously I untied the ribbon, pulled away the blue gift wrapping and took out an alarm clock cushioned in bubble wrap. A handwritten note clung to the clock.

Dear Rabbi,

This clock has been set for fifteen minutes. If your sermon extends beyond the allotted time the alarm will ring, and ring, and ring: until you stop speaking. Sorry to do this to you but fifteen minutes should be long enough for any sermon!

Best wishes and good luck.

The Timekeeper!

This was not a dream. This was a nightmare! Imagine, asking a clergyman to limit his words to fifteen minutes! Fifteen, fourteen, thirteen, twelve.

I awoke in the morning bathed in sweat. Why? Because I sensed the dream was not about sermons. The dream was about life. What if, what if, instead of being granted only fifteen minutes for a sermon I had fifteen minutes to live? Or fifteen years? Or fifty one? The allotment is never sufficient.

Sobered by this understanding I asked myself: How had I used my time? How many minutes, even years, had I squandered? And although I could not redeem lost time, how could I enrich the remaining years? Settling into a soft leather chair, accompanied by an alarm clock and the faith that I do not have to be the passive victim of time's relentless pursuit, I began to reassess my life.

Since everything that happens to a rabbi eventually finds its way into a sermon, I decided to share the dream with my congregation at a High Holy Day service. The response was positive. One individual commented: "I just wanted to let you know how thought provoking your sermon was last night. The alarm clock that limited you to fifteen minutes is a concept that I have thought about many times—at the service I expected to hear pleas for everyone to seek forgiveness for what they had done wrong and promises not to do it again. What you said instead (or perhaps in addition) was live life to the fullest—to me, this is solid practical advice too often ignored before the alarm sounds."

A New York investment banker, who conquered cancer in recent months, wrote: "This letter is to compliment you on the sermon relating to time and how precious it really is. After listening to it, many in our family discussed how relevant it was, not only to us but to everyone who heard it. We obviously didn't have the power to start the clock running, nor the power to keep it running, but as you so poignantly stated, we have the ability to make the most of the time we do have."

To make the most of the time we have. That is really what this book is about, what life is about. And, after receiving the varied comments I embarked on a more extensive project, asking congregants, friends, students, "If you only had a limited time to live but were in good health and could do whatever you want what would you do?" I set an arbitrary time limit of two years, but the actual amount of time is unimportant. The question is important. "How would you reprioritize time if there were only a brief span stretching before you?" In other words, "Would you make changes in your life if you knew you only had two years? Or one year, or five years?" And now for my conclusion. (I love chapters that begin with conclusions!) Your time *is* limited. Simple as that! We hope to enjoy a lifetime rich in years but we will never have enough time. I remember spotting one of those wonderful little ads at the bottom of the first page of the *New York Times*; one-liners that say "Suzie, I love you"; "12 Fifth Avenue has been liberated from the cable monopoly." But the ad that resonated said "B.J. I want more. C.F." We always want more, especially of life. We never have enough, but we can use the time granted to us constructively and reap a rich harvest. Aware of limits we maximize how we will live within those limits, not only for two years but for the many years to follow.

This final part, "You Only Live Twice", includes the responses to my inquiry into the use of time. Hopefully the thoughts of others will stimulate you to reprioritize your own life—if necessary. Then, two years from now, when you look back and once again ask, "Where have I been all my Life?", you will smile and say, "I made the most of these years. They have been filled with happiness, contentment, and love."

Dear Rabbi,

I would tell everyone, 'You only live twice.' Then they would appreciate the brevity of only living once.

Sam

Dear Rabbi,

If I only had two years to live I wouldn't think about it, because then I would realize I only had two years to live.

If I only had two years to live I would—live.

Robin

Sitting with Don on the porch of his 1803 cottage next to a pond covered with water lilies he spoke about his home.

"Marge and I fell in love with this house when we were thirty—used to be a farmer's cottage. The white picket fence, ivy covering the Stone garage, wild raspberries—how could you not love this cottage?"

I nodded.

"We had one hesitation. The downstairs ceilings measured five feet ten inches between the beams. Only guests five feet nine inches and less could enter. That eliminated my brother-in-law. I might add that this factor only increased the appeal. By 5:00 P.M. the next day we had a verbal agreement with the owners."

Don smiled as he reminisced.

"On moving day the movers, Ben and Ray, twisted and turned as they carried the king size mattress up the low-slung staircase, swore as they brought the old oak table into the dining room and hit their heads on the ceiling. By late morning the pair had finished off a six-pack of beer and were flipping the furniture like the short order cooks in the Chappaqua diner. Only one piece of furniture remained on the truck, a grandfather clock that my great-grandmother Sybil brought from England in the 1850s.

Each dent in the oak casing represented another chapter in a family saga beginning in Salem, Massachusetts. 'Careful!' I called out as the movers carried the clock wrapped in a dark green packing quilt.

"'What you got here, Buddy, a body?' Ben asked.

"'No, just a grandfather clock. Goes over there. By the fireplace.'

"Suddenly Marge gasped. 'Don, the clock's too tall for the ceiling.' She was right.

"Ben, halfway into his second six-pack, suggested cutting a hole in the ceiling; Ray voted for a hole in the floor and Marge suggested we build an enclosure for the clock on the front porch. 'That way when the neighbors walk by they can pass the time of day.' I was not in the mood for humor.

"Rummaging through my tool chest I found a saw. To my wife's horror and the moving men's delight I cut two inches off the four spindles on top of the clock. The clock fit perfectly. Over the years we have laughed about my skill as a surgeon. Marge explains to company, 'In 1953 Don cut his old grandfather back to size.' Of a more philosophical bent I point out, 'I was only cutting back on time.'

"With two years to live I would search for a way to lengthen time, or, at least use time well and I would never cut back on time—anymore than was absolutely necessary."

Jim, a congregant in his mid-forties, soft spoken and pensive, occasionally attended adult education classes but seldom offered comments. Although a member for many years I never had a reading of this man who spent his days as an accountant in a family business in White Plains. Then, last year, as we discussed the quote from the biblical Book of Psalms "This is the day the Lord has made. Rejoice and be glad in it," Jim seemed troubled. Later in the evening he approached me.

"Dan, the words 'this is the day' triggers a memory." I nodded.

"I was twenty-nine," he continued. "My closest friend Bob had died. One of those rugged athletic men, always pushing himself. He had gone for his physical in the morning, left the doctor's office and jogged nine miles, his usual distance. The next day the doctor called, something in the blood test he didn't like. Nine months later Bob died. Leukemia.

"Following the funeral I attended the reading of the will. While Mr. Hessberg, the lawyer, read the bequests my thoughts wandered to experiences Bob and I had shared. We grew up on South Main, attended P.S. 19, climbed garage roofs as kids, rock cliffs near Lake Placid as adults.

"After some moments Mr. Hessberg turned toward me."

"'Jim, your friend has left you an unusual legacy.'

> To Jim, I leave the memories of time shared. I also bequeath to my friend since childhood the years I never had, with the desire that he will live for both of us.
>
> Witnessed this 5th day of March, 1987.

Jim paused. "Of course, on that day when the will was read, I knew Bob could not give away his unfulfilled future. It was not his to bequeath. But I sensed Bob was telling me something else: 'Jim, no one is promised tomorrow. Live for today. Then you will live for both of us.'

"Dan, that is how I will live my years."

I would find happiness in common things.

I would follow the advice of André Gide and "enjoy this summer flower by flower, as if it were to be the last one for me."

Dear Dan,

I would volunteer at the Botanical Garden. I have always loved anything that blossoms.

Sarah

Dear Dan,

I always leave everything to the last minute, and finish just under the deadline. Any enjoyment I might feel from completing a task becomes lost in the last minute pressure. Now, even the word "deadline" disturbs me.

In the future I intend to be early.

I mentioned the subject of time to my cousin Burt while he patted his stomach and salivated longingly over a menu at the Stage Deli on Broadway. Dreams of New York corned beef sandwiches, potato salad, and cheesecake warmed the cold Minneapolis winters where Burt lived and when the Northwest Airlines flight landed at La Guardia Airport, Burt almost forgave our grandfather, a tailor turned Minnesota State Fair barker, for the frontier spirit that landed our family three thousand miles from the Stage Deli.

After sixty years Burt has perfected the fine art of eating. For instance, he wears eye glasses to read the menu. The glasses, attached behind his ears with elastic bands, rest on his chest and point upwards like two saucers. As he devours a hot buttered croissant crumbs fall onto his glasses. By the last course Burt's glasses have trapped a respectable supply of leftovers that Burt then scoops up for an after dinner snack.

The only obstacle between Burt and food is Rusty, his caring wife, who creates diets faster than Burt invents diet busting techniques. The 73rd and most recent diet included broiled sole, one slab of dry toast and seltzer. Therefore, Burt did not hesitate when I inquired, "If you only had two years . . .?" Without missing a beat or a bite Burt mumbled, "I would eat whatever I wanted."

And he smiled.

Dear Rabbi,

Next to my screen porch a verbena grows. There are many varieties of this bush but mine boasts dark buds in late April. They brush against the windows when the wind blows and then, on the first warm day of spring, burst open, revealing white blossoms flushed with pink. For many years I viewed these flowers from afar but last year I opened the windows and the rich scent of the verbena drifted in through the windows, gradually enveloping the entire house. I spent my days draped in their lovely fragrance.

If I had two years I would open windows and invite the outside in.

Sincerely,
Monique

Dear Dan,
I would stop saying:
take your time
find the time
make the time
In peace,
Sister Mary Campion

Ken's apartment bulged with adventure travel catalogs, Gore-Tex boots from Eastern Mountain Sports and a collection of walking sticks from every continent. Fortunately, Ken's wife Nancy shared his love of exotic travel. They were married on camels in the Sahara Desert. Even the birth of Samarra did not deter this wanderlust. Packing up their daughter, Ken and Nancy sailed for six months off the coast of Turkey then circled home through Armenia. I was not surprised when Ken said he would spend his two years traveling.

"Where would you go?" I asked.

Ken smiled and stroked a red beard touched by the first traces of gray.

"Paris. For a boat trip on the Seine."

I looked puzzled. "A boat trip on the Seine? What happened to your sense of adventure? Haven't you ever been on the Seine?"

"Sure," Ken laughed. "Thirty years ago. We took one of those tourist boats from the Quai d'Orsay. Two hundred people crowded onto the deck for a fifty-minute tour. A great night. A full moon. The guides voice announced, 'Mesdames and Monsieurs, on your left the Louvre. Built in the thirteenth century. Home of the Mona Lisa.' A giant spotlight illuminated the stone facade and I was wandering back into the past when suddenly the light left the Louvre and flashed onto the Palais de Justice. Then the boat cut through the waters and we were at Notre Dame. Years later I still remember the spotlight flitting from building to building on the sixty-minute tour. You can't imagine how quickly we passed through history. Each time I wanted to settle in the guides voice interrupted: 'And now, on your right. And now, on your left.'

"If I only had two years I would return to the Seine to remind myself that time does not stop and if I don't follow the moving light I will be left in darkness."

Dear Dan,

Since your letter arrived it has remained on my desk, an uninvited guest greeted with less than complete enthusiasm. It raises some troublesome questions which I have struggled with many times, and have yet to answer to my satisfaction. I am a firm believer in the Socratic method and as you anticipated it is far easier to pose questions than to arrive at their answers. Indeed, if I knew the "answers" as they related to me, I would be celebrating and therefore too occupied to answer your letter. Unfortunately that is not the case.

As I have gotten older and experienced the loss or illness of family and friends, it has become more difficult to avoid the question of "what if . . .". Each spring, in what must be a self imposed male macho rite, I don my wet suit and go wind surfing prior to my birthday in May. The water is usually chilling and the wind surfing quite brief. Once completed I congratulate myself that I was able to do it for yet another year. The same ritual applies to my annual ski trip out West.

I see a connection between these rituals and the increasing need to prioritize my life, for they underscore the transient nature of existence and the fleeting opportunity we have to celebrate it. I am forced to consider what's important, what's real, what's just and what is righteous.

Dick

Dear Rabbi,

I would try to program in more than 52 Sundays. I love the Sunday crossword puzzle, and the thought of only 104 more Sundays—well, that's pretty depressing both up and down.

Jim

Dear Dan,

Let me tell you about a trip to Israel that I will never forget. On the night of the full moon the Society for the Preservation of Nature in Israel conducted a walking tour in the wadis, the dry riverbeds of the Judaean desert. I had joined twenty hikers who clamored off the bus, water bottles thrust into backpacks and flashlights ready for the nighttime hike towards Jericho, oldest city in the world. Three thousand years earlier Joshua had followed this route when he entered the Promised Land. Except Joshua walked by daylight! Lights from Israeli settlements and army bases flickered in the distance, illuminating a barren moonscape of hills. This was not the portion of Israel flowing with milk and honey! Turning on my flashlight I followed the ray of light, tentatively picking my way over boulders and clefts in the hillside. Up ahead our guide, Gideon, slipped over the rough terrain like a mountain goat. I fell further and further behind.

Gideon approached: "Dan, can you walk faster? It took the children of Israel forty years but the bus expects us in Jericho at midnight."

"Not easy, Gideon. I don't want to trip and this flashlight's not powerful."

A grin spread across Gideon's face shining in the moonlight.

"Why not put the flashlight away. Here, I'll stuff it in your backpack."

I protested. "Then everything will be black."

"Trust me," Gideon said. Afraid of being left in the desert, I followed his advice and flicked off the light. Immediately a broad panorama opened up, freed from the shadows cast by the artificial light. I could see! There in the distance was Jericho; along the way boulders and an occasional acacia tree.

I caught up with the group near St. Georges Monastery, the massive Greek Orthodox retreat built into rocks cliffs above the wadi. Soon, at 4:00 A.M., the monks would rise for prayer and invoke God's name. "Kyrie, Kyrie," the furtive wail holding the desert captive. The monks believed God watched over them, showing the way into the wilderness. They might be correct. But at that moment I traveled without help. Not even a flashlight. This was one of those moments when my own resources proved most helpful.

If I knew I only had two years to live I would treasure the support of those who care about me but I would determine

the direction of my life, what I would do and how I would do it. I would be my own light. Aren't we the arbiters of our lives?
Sincerely,
Max

I would rush for the phone and tell people I love them.
Jimmy

Dan,
I would like people to spend those two years saying nice things about me; the thoughts they might express in a eulogy. Why shouldn't I be around to hear?
Joseph P.

Dear Rabbi,
I've been on a pretty fast track these past years and haven't had much time to be with family; especially my Grandpa Ned. Grandpa and I were really close when I was young. We went to Yankee games together. Trout fishing.
He hasn't been well and he would have loved to have seen me. But he never made demands. Then, last week I heard he was dying and I rushed up to White Plains. It was my last visit with Grandfather. I'll tell you, Rabbi, if I only had two years I wouldn't wait until the end to visit those I care about. No, I wouldn't wait until the end.
Sincerely,
Roger

I sat with Jean in the courtyard of the Albright Institute. Jean had recently returned from her home in Oklahoma City. Pensively Jean searched a cypress tree where morning doves hid in the thick branches.

"Dan, I never replied to your question, 'If you only had two years to live.' You asked me that, when was it, three months ago, before my parents came?"

Jean's parents had visited Israel for ten days over the Christmas period, "To see our children and the Christian holy places." Both Jean and her husband Evan had not looked forward to the visit. There was stress when everyone was together and this trip was no exception.

Jean's father after a visit to Bethlehem: "How can you have a white Christmas when the temperature's seventy degrees?"

Jean's mother after a morning touring the archeological collection at the Israel Museum: "I've seen better pottery at Bloomingdales!"

Evan's father-in-law almost deleted two years of Evan's dissertation on the Minoan civilization when he pressed the wrong key on the computer. Jean's mom complained when she could not order a ham sandwich in a kosher restaurant.

The litany continued. A family argument in the Trappist monastery where monks had taken vows of silence; a dent in the Renault when Jean's father accidentally backed into a tank on the Golan Heights. . . .

"But when it was all over," Evan admitted, "the folks had a wonderful time. I'm glad they came. This really was a once in a lifetime experience for them and we feel good about the visit."

Evan and Jean could not realize at that moment the truth of their comment, "A once in a lifetime experience." Three months later, driving on a rain slick road outside of Oklahoma City, Jean's parents were killed in an automobile accident. When Jean returned home to attend to her parents affairs she saw a living-room filled with photographs of the vacation in Israel: buying an olive wood cross in front of the Church of the Holy Sepulcher, climbing down from the Roman fortress at Masada, dancing on the pedestrian mall with a Jew from the Soviet Union and a poster-size picture of the family hugging at the departure gate of Ben Gurion Airport.

Now, as a lone morning dove swooped from the tree, Jean said softly, "I miss my parents terribly but I don't have regrets about inviting them to visit. They saw Israel. They saw us. I think we only regret what we do not do. If I had two years I would spend a portion of the time following up on what I said I would do—and haven't done."

Dear Dan,

Time and I are moving in inverse proportion. The older I become (and the slower I walk) the faster time seems to move. If I only had two years I would try to stay the pace of time although I know this is impossible.

When my children left for college I joked with my husband, "Well Dear, now we have that room for your study." But I couldn't wait for David and Phoebe to come home for a visit. Even with their dirty laundry. Then David married, accepted a job in Dayton and I was too far away to be part of my granddaughter Suzie's first day at school. They sent a picture. Then little Joel telephoned, "Granny, I lost my tooth and I can ride my three-wheeler. Come see me." But the distance is great, the visits too brief, and now you tell me I only have two years.

Well, I promise to enjoy those visits even more than I already do—unless someone can tell me how to stop time.

Sincerely,

Sophie Caitlin

I would delight in the smiles of my children.

It is natural at the birth of a child to envision his or her future, but occasionally we plan too far in advance. This was evident when I received a birth announcement on glossy vellum with a blue border rimming black letters:

REBECCA & BEN WINOKER

TAKE PLEASURE IN ANNOUNCING

THE BIRTH OF THEIR SON

DR. SCOTT WINOKER

7 LBS. 9 OUNCES

(That announcement was sent in the days when every parent wanted their son to be a doctor. To be more precise—in the days before HMOs)

The announcement tied into a letter I received from Grace Berthold, a college advisor at a leading private school in the Metropolitan area.

Dear Rabbi,

I will answer your query from my own personal perspective based on an interview with a Mrs. Deborah Farber. She barged into my office without an appointment the first day of the school year.

"It's urgent, Mrs. Berthold," she began. "Please, I have a few questions."

"Can they wait?" l asked

"No, please, I'll Just take a minute."

I settled back and listened.

"Mrs. Berthold," Deborah began, "This college admissions pressure! I'm so worried about Samantha I haven't slept in a week. Maybe you can answer my questions:

"Where do most of your students go to college?

"What books do you advise for improving SAT scores?

"Does the high school provide tutors?

"How important is a cheerleading letter or work experience in a local boutique?

"What colleges have the best entry records for medical school?"

I was puzzled. "Excuse me, Mrs. Farber, I thought I knew all my parents but I don't remember you from any of our meetings and I don't remember your daughter, Samantha."

Mrs. Farber laughed. "Oh, Mrs. Berthold, Samantha isn't enrolled in your school, at least not yet. We don't even live here, but Oscar and I are considering buying a house in this school district and I simply had to know the answers to these questions. After all, Samantha is entering first grade, and we want to make sure she'll be well prepared!"

"Mrs. Farber," I asked, "aren't you in a bit of a rush? I realize you wish the very best for Samantha but before she applies to college in twelve years wouldn't it be wise to enjoy grades one through eleven? In other words, you have reached the end before considering the beginning and the middle. What about the grades along the way?

If Mrs. Farber only had two years to live I hope she would enjoy the years before college with Samantha. That's what I would do.

Sincerely,
Grace Berthold

Dear Rabbi,

Because of your question, in June, my son in Vermont with his newish wife and stepdaughter, my newly divorced son in Denver, and my son and his wife in New York, plus me will all be flying to a week's vacation at a Club Med in the Caribbean.

Thank you for starting a thinking process that has brought,

or will bring, children and grandchildren together and I'll be there to enjoy it. The most amazing aspect of this family gathering is it's not for a funeral!

With thanks,
Paula

Sherry and I stood outside my office waiting for Peter to complete Confirmation class, the tenth grade in our religious school.

"Sherry, if you only had two years to live how would you spend your time?"

Her face darkened.

"I would spend more time with Peter; involve myself in his interests—if he allowed. Get all the family together. Weekend excursions, dinner together. That sort of thing."

Then Sherry's face brightened. "But, since I have forty, maybe fifty years to live, I'll tell you quite honestly—I can't wait until Peter leaves for college and takes his stereo with him!"

Dear Dan,

As you are aware, my wife Claire did not have two years to live. The doctors were quite clear—six months, maximum a year. But there was no doubt what Claire would do; take Becky to Paris.

In our family we had a tradition. Whenever a grandchild graduated from high school we would travel with them to Europe. Becky was the last of the grandchildren and we scheduled a week in Paris for mid-August. The two weeks before departure Claire stayed in bed most of the day to gather strength. On a bright summer morning we departed Kennedy Airport with Becky, two suitcases and every prescription imaginable from pain killers to blood thinners.

Looking back I don't know how Claire made it through the week. Hours in the Louvre, an afternoon at Versailles, the

Cathedral at Chartres, a boat trip on the Seine, etc. The first day Becky kept saying to her grandmother, "Nana, you have to rest," but Claire would have none of that although at Giverny she spent an extra hour sketching water lilies. By 8:00 P.M. she had slumped onto her pillow but each morning she was ready for another day.

August 19th. That was the day we returned to New York. Descending the steps of the Air France jet Claire saw Becky's father, Mort, and gave a thumbs up gesture. All I could think of was John Donne, "Death thou shalt die." On August 29th you officiated at Claire's funeral and Becky, in her eulogy, told her Nana, "You will always be with me. You have not died. Wherever I go l will take you with me—and I will think of Paris."

Now, as a proxy for my beloved Claire, permit me to answer your question. If I only had two years to live, or six months, I would make every moment an affirmation of life and I would touch those closest to me—that I might not die.

Sincerely,

Richard, on behalf of Claire.

Dear Rabbi Wolk,

I was impressed with the fact that your advice to us all was based on how to live positively and as the song says to make hay while the sun shines. In my job, I moved from NYC to Harrison four and a half years ago to avoid the hassles of the commute, to be able to coach the kids in various sports and to be able to spend more time with them. Since that time, I have been asked repeatedly to return to New York, which would certainly reduce the time I could spend with the kids. While it cost me a promotion or two, I have turned them down and probably confused the management a bit. Nonetheless, I see the clock ticking. I see a time when the kids will be on their own and the main focus of my life will have to change.

Thanks for your thoughts.

Sincerely,

John

Dear Dan,

I considered your question yesterday on the 6:09 from Mount Kisco to Grand Central. That's the train I have taken to work for ten years. I leave the house at dawn. I'm back in time to kiss Jared good night. The train stopped at Chappaqua, Pleasantville, White Plains, Scarsdale, 125th Street. Suddenly each station was a stop in Jared's life. A Little League game, the school play, the day he asked me to take him trick or treating. I didn't have time to stop for Jared; I was on the express train in my own life. Now I cannot go back. What did I miss? Insignificant stations? Or the journey of a son growing up?

In the future I will take the local, arrive at work later, come home earlier and share Jared's life.

Sincerely,
Ed

Dear Daniel,

Your intriguing letter of October 14th gave us considerable pause. I feel your question is so difficult that I cannot answer it in any but the most conventional way.

I did see a one-liner recently on this subject, which I am passing along to you. It was an ad for a family magazine and the headline was, "On Your Deathbed, You Probably Won't Regret Not Having Spent More Time with the Company Controller."

Sincerely,
Michael

Dear Dan,
I would leave my briefcase at the office.
Horace

I would try and cheer up somebody else, then I would also be cheered.

M.F.

Dear Rabbi,

When I was young my parents brought me jumping beans from a trip to Mexico. I took them outside and sat on a park bench but they wouldn't jump; like my slinky toy that wouldn't slink down the steps, and the yo-yo that settled for a one way trip—down. I was toy illiterate. Why should the jumping beans jump?

I sat on the bench, staring at the beans. Nothing. Then my father took the beans into the sunlight and after a few minutes the beans popped and hopped. My father explained they come alive when they are warm; on the bench it was too cool and shady.

If I had two years to live I would bring warmth to others. Give them life.

Cara

Dear Dan,

The most difficult decision would be whether to turn inward or outward. I would hope for the strength of spirit to avoid the temptation to taste every postponed pleasure. Beyond that I would hope to do more than immerse myself within a loving family circle; although I would certainly want to spend more and more intense time with those closest to me.

As a lawyer, perhaps my first effort would be to work more intensely and with an emphasis on the human elements always involved in legal projects. My leitmotif would be doing good rather than looking good.

Alan

Dear Rabbi,

For five years I have practiced medicine. When a patient asks a question I am prepared with a detailed answer, usually giving more information than the patient wants to hear; the blood count, protein level, sugars. Sometimes I discuss possible treatment: Radiation. Chemo. An exploratory operation. Why do I give these details? Probably to protect myself, but also it is easier to take refuge behind facts than to deal with people.

My father, Abe, was a family practitioner; the kind that paid house calls. Remember that breed of doctor? He carried far less knowledge than modern doctors; only a little black bag, a soft presence, and a gentle touch. Those were his medicines. Whenever I'm in Albany and visit my parent's grave someone always says, "Aren't you Dr. Abe's son?" That's the only place in the world where someone sees me as "Dr. Abe's son." Then they usually add. "He healed with his heart."

We've made so many advances in the field of medicine. Discoveries my father never dreamed of. Most people don't want to know about technical advances. That's important for their body, not for their soul.

In the next two years I will answer the patient's question, not my needs, and—I will give fewer facts and more hope.

Sincerely,
Stuart

Dan,

I have found one of the worst wastes of time is quarreling with family and friends; therefore I would quickly resolve disputes.

My best,
Nicole

Dear Dan,

I recall a statement made many times by my father and grandmother: "Be a mench." It seems to say it all.

Bernie

Dear Dan,

I read that the average college student watches 21 hours of television each week. Many adults watch even more. With limited time I would hope to be a doer instead of a spectator.

Sincerely,

Erica L.

Dear Rabbi,

The poet Keats, a year before his death at the age of 25, wrote "If I should die I have left no immortal work behind me . . . but I have laid the principle of beauty of all things and if I had time I would have made myself remembered."

I would try to find some way to be remembered.

Larry

Dear Dan,

Photographs of Martha's Vineyard hang on the walls of my den; seagulls diving into the surf, the sun setting on a sailboat, my blonde haired daughter Hannah picking daisies, our weather-beaten gray house outside Edgartown. The pictures capture thirty summers on the vineyard. They trace my family's growth and my happiness.

With two years to live I would gaze at the photos every morning, to remind myself where I have been and the fullness of my life. This would be a time to gaze backwards.

Yours,

Laura

I spoke with my compassionate friend Meera on the porch of a cottage in a tea plantation in the south of India. She explained her concept of time. Wrapping a shawl around her shoulders she began:

"Every year I visit my family. I come here from Calcutta, to sit in this valley and look out at these mountains." Then she asked me, "What do you see?"

A formation of geese followed the stream, their wings reflecting on the light brown water below. "The mountains," I answered, "Rising on either side."

"And?" Meera asked.

I was silent.

"The mountains on the west are in shadow," she continued, "the mountains on the east catch the midafternoon sun."

I nodded.

"I come here because, when one range of mountains is in shadow the other is in light. Then they change roles as the sun passes overhead. That's the way it is with life. Nothing is always dark. Nothing is always light. Once a year I sit on this porch to remind myself that life is a balance. The sun. The shadows. Neither lasts forever. When I return to Calcutta I bring this image with me and focus somewhere in the middle. When life is bright I can enjoy the happiness. When life is dark I am reassured.

"No matter how many years I have I would tell myself life is a balance of sunlight and shadows. This thought brings me peace."

Because the young believe they will live forever they rush time. "When will my birthday ever come," a seven year old asks on the Monday before he turns eight. "When will I grow," the four feet eleven inch wannabe Michael Jordan asks. Why does it take so many years to have my braces removed or an eternity before I can drive? Why? Why? Why does time move this slowly?

But occasionally life intrudes in harsh unwelcome ways and the force of death touches those whose life is only beginning. One such incident precipitated the following letter, adapted from an essay on a college application written by a high school senior in Westchester.

Dear Rabbi,

When I was thirteen my friend Sharon was killed skiing. She was cut off on an expert trail in Vermont, slipped on a patch of ice and went into a tree. She died instantly. One moment we were kids, jumping over moguls and the next moment. . . .

Now, as I meet each new experience I tell myself, "Sharon never got to do this. She never knew what it was like to be in high school, go to a prom, see Europe, climb in the Rockies. She never kissed a boy, fell in love, applied to college, or watched Seinfeld." Each day I live is one more day than she lived. I never forget that, and I really appreciate my life.

Sincerely,

Dara

The following responses were written by members of the senior class at School of The Holy Child. Some of the most sensitive replies came from girls who seemed uninterested in the educational experience, but, on a deeper level their minds were well honed and their hearts sensitive. I would hope that those whose spark has not been kindled by formal education will realize the world sparkles with the promise of many possibilities. The challenge consists of discovering the area proper for you. At any age.

To think about what I would do if I had two years to live, scares me. You have to face the fact that you will be dead soon and won't be able to see your children grow or just fulfill your life in general. I just wouldn't want to sleep. I would always want to be doing things. I am just the type of person that would not be able to sit around and watch everything go before me. I wouldn't feel sorry for myself, and sob in my room. I would just try to do the best in life and have fun.

Anne

All in all I would get as much as I could out of life, and not let a day pass without accomplishing something.

Amy

The next individual, Danielle, reminds me of the movie Honey, I Shrunk The Kids *except the movie of her two years might be entitled* Honey, I Shrunk The Time. *Evident in her comments is the philosophy of diversifying life; living on multidimensional levels. This advice echoes with a universal resonance.*

If I only had two years to live I would try to pack as much fun into my life while I could. I would go to college, but live closer to home so I could be with my family and friends. At college I would try to become friends with lots of people right away, and I would only take courses in subjects that are of interest to me.

I'd try to travel and see as much of the world as I could, and I wouldn't worry about spending lots of money. I'd buy people gifts constantly and shop just for fun. I'd also do scary things like hang gliding and mountain climbing. I'd go out with a different guy every night until I found someone I really liked and then I'd spend lots of time with him. I would definitely rent a house on a beautiful beach and just spend hours swimming and in the sun. If I only had two years to live I would try to do good things for others in my family and I would volunteer to help the poor so that I would know I was doing something positive to make the world a better place.

Danielle

Besides just doing things in my two years of remaining life, I would also think and feel differently. Every moment that I would spend with my friends and family would be that much more precious. I would be so much kinder to people I normally wasn't as nice to. I would learn to value my most important relationships, with my parents, my brother and my best friends. I think I would probably become more charitable—I would volunteer more, and donate most of the money that I didn't need—it's not like I would be saving for retirement or anything.

Jennifer

There is one other thing in the city that I have always wanted to do. I see so many homeless people, but I never know which ones spend money on liquor and drugs and which ones really need help. I find it very difficult to understand. If I knew I was going to die, my money would not do me any good once dead, so I would spend it. I would like to put a dollar in every cup of every homeless person I saw live in the city. I guess that sounds silly, but I have always wanted to do it.

Brenda

For the first year, I would work hard to find the ultimate cure for the common cold. Aside from that I'd write a book entitled, "How to Live Like a Sunflower." That way even if I die, I could technically still live. And that way I could earn some money to blow in my last year of existence.

Melissa

One thing I have always wanted to do is volunteer at a nursing home; however, I have yet to take the initiative. It has been too easy to make excuses as to why I couldn't. If I knew I was going to die, then I would make the time to work there. Some of my happiest memories are of the times I spent taking care of my grandfather when I lived with him before he died. I would like to spend some of my last moments with older people who aren't fortunate enough to be at home with their families. I thank God that my grandfather was lucky enough to be able to die at home with the people who loved him. I Just wish that all people could be that lucky. Older people are usually happy and have such nice stories and memories to share. I would like to spend time with them hearing about these things. I don't like the idea of the elderly being left alone in nursing homes. My spending time with them would be a lot of fun for me and hopefully for them.

    Kristina

I think one decision I would make would be to quit school. I have always looked at life as a cycle of continual learning and sharing this learning with others. If I only had two years to live, I would spend this time sharing what I've learned already.

    Caroline

If I had only two years left to live I would try to better prepare myself for my afterlife, which I hope will be in Heaven. I do not think I would want to tell my loved ones because I would not want them to worry. I might, however, go to a priest for spiritual counseling and moral support. I would not let myself mope around in self-pity for the special things in life which I would miss, such as marriage, having children, seeing grandchildren. It would be hard, but for the most part I think that I would try not to think about dying at all.

    Darlene

* * *

Dear Rabbi,

    I would not accept your premise that I only had two years to live. Last Christmas I delivered a sermon on the need for faith.

One of the illustrations I used was the story of a man imprisoned in an Eastern European kingdom during medieval times. The death sentence had been decreed and, in a final attempt to save his life, the prisoner petitioned the king.

"Your Highness, what must I do to live?"

The king replied, "Teach my horse to talk."

The suppliant considered the terms. "I can teach your horse to speak but I will need fifteen years."

After some hesitation the king agreed and brought the prisoner to his stable where he would live next to the horse.

When the king's servants heard of the bargain they approached the man.

"Fool! How could you make such a promise to the king?"

The man replied. "It is not foolish. In fifteen years the king may die, I may die or," and a twinkle came into his eyes, "I may teach the horse to talk."

Dan, I believe anything is possible and I would live defying the two-year decree. Who knows how long we may live, when we may die?

I hope this reply is helpful.

Father Kevin

Two years? That's not the scenario I would have written but I suppose I would play it as best I can.

I would learn to live with broken dreams.

While asking individuals how they would prioritize time I met Jean at the local stationery store. Jean was browsing through a stack of filofax. Since I exist on handwritten notes (that I can never find) I asked Jean about her approach to organization.

Jean straightened her neatly pressed gray Neiman-Marcus suit and glancing at her watch explained her philosophy of careful planning. "Buy a filofax." She flipped through her red leather book divided into "Diary," "Projects," "Information," and "Financial." Notes filled every corner with barely a speck of white paper peeking out beneath the neatly inscribed handwriting. "My life!" Jean beamed as she thrust the filofax in my direction. Reluctant to take someone else's life in my hands I declined her offer.

"Every morning and evening I devote time to my filofax; planning the days, the weeks. I can tell you where I will be at 7:00 A.M., February 20th, two months from now. If anything happened to my filofax I would be lost."

Impressed by this woman's control of time I asked, "Jean, if you only had two years to live, in other words two more orders of blank filofax pages, would you plan differently?" For a moment her filofax quivered in her hand, then, regaining her composure and replacing a gray strand of hair into the neat bun on the back of her head she answered: "If I only had two years to live I might spend less time planning, more time living."